DATE DUE			

30408000006018

327.1
WEA

Weapons of mass
destruction

Woodland High School
HENRY COUNTY PUBLIC SCHOOLS

INTRODUCING
ISSUES WITH
OPPOSING
VIEWPOINTS®

Weapons
of Mass
Destruction

Other books in the Introducing Issues
with Opposing Viewpoints series:

Abortion
Advertising
AIDS
Alcohol
Animal Rights
Civil Liberties
Cloning
The Death Penalty
Drug Abuse
Drunk Driving
Energy Alternatives
The Environment
Euthanasia
Gangs
Gay Marriage
Genetic Engineering
Global Warming
Gun Control
Illegal Immigration
Islam
Marijuana
The Middle East
Military Draft
Obesity
Pollution
Racism
Smoking
Teen Pregnancy
Terrorism
UFOs

INTRODUCING
ISSUES WITH
OPPOSING
VIEWPOINTS®

Weapons
of Mass
Destruction

Lauri S. Friedman, *Book Editor*

Christine Nasso, *Publisher*
Elizabeth Des Chenes, *Managing Editor*

WOODLAND HIGH SCHOOL
800 N. MOSELEY DRIVE
STOCKBRIDGE, GA 30281
(770) 389-2784

GREENHAVEN PRESS
An imprint of Thomson Gale, a part of The Thomson Corporation

THOMSON
™
GALE

Detroit • New York • San Francisco • New Haven, Conn. • Waterville, Maine • London

LIBRARY OF CONGRESS CATALOGING-IN-PUBLICATION DATA

Weapons of mass destruction / Lauri S. Friedman, book editor.
  p. cm. — (Introducing issues with opposing viewpoints)
 Includes bibliographical references and index.
 ISBN-13: 978-0-7377-3617-5 (hc)
 1. Weapons of mass destruction. I. Friedman, Lauri S.
 U793.W4263 2007
 327.1'745—dc22

                                    2007006074

ISBN-10: 0-7377-3617-8
Printed in the United States of America

Contents

Foreword   7

Introduction   9

Chapter 1: Do Weapons of Mass Destruction Pose a Serious Threat?

1. The U.S. Is Likely to Be Attacked with Weapons of   14
   Mass Destruction
   Harold Kennedy

2. The U.S. Is Not Likely to Be Attacked with Weapons of   20
   Mass Destruction
   William M. Arkin

3. Iraq Possessed Weapons of Mass Destruction   27
   Rick Santorum and Peter Hoekstra

4. Iraq Did Not Possess Weapons of Mass Destruction   34
   Alan Reynolds

Chapter 2: How Can the Spread of Weapons of Mass Destruction Be Prevented?

1. The Nuclear Non-Proliferation Treaty Can Prevent the   41
   Spread of Weapons of Mass Destruction
   Stephen G. Rademaker

2. The Nuclear Non-Proliferation Treaty Cannot Prevent the   48
   Spread of Weapons of Mass Destruction
   Liaquat Ali Khan

3. International Cooperation Will Prevent the Spread of   55
   Weapons of Mass Destruction
   George W. Bush

4. Nothing Can Prevent the Spread of Weapons of Mass   62
   Destruction
   William Langewiesche

Chapter 3: How Should Rogue Nations Who Seek Weapons of Mass Destruction Be Dealt With?

1. Military Action Could Prevent Iran from Acquiring Weapons of Mass Destruction   69
   William Kristol

2. Military Action Should Not Be Undertaken Against Iran   75
   M.M. Eskandari-Qajar

3. Sanctions Will Force North Korea to Give Up Its Weapons of Mass Destruction   81
   United Nations Security Council Draft Resolution 1718

4. Sanctions Will Not Force North Korea to Give Up Its Weapons of Mass Destruction   88
   Nicholas D. Kristof

5. Diplomacy Will Force North Korea to Give Up Its Weapons of Mass Destruction   93
   Robert L. Gallucci

6. Bribery Will Force North Korea to Give Up Its Weapons of Mass Destruction   99
   Gwynne Dyer

Facts About Weapons of Mass Destruction   105

Glossary   110

Organizations to Contact   113

For Further Reading   119

Index   124

Picture Credits   128

Foreword

Indulging in a wide spectrum of ideas, beliefs, and perspectives is a critical cornerstone of democracy. After all, it is often debates over differences of opinion, such as whether to legalize abortion, how to treat prisoners, or when to enact the death penalty, that shape our society and drive it forward. Such diversity of thought is frequently regarded as the hallmark of a healthy and civilized culture. As the Reverend Clifford Schutjer of the First Congregational Church in Mansfield, Ohio, declared in a 2001 sermon, "Surrounding oneself with only like-minded people, restricting what we listen to or read only to what we find agreeable is irresponsible. Refusing to entertain doubts once we make up our minds is a subtle but deadly form of arrogance." With this advice in mind, Introducing Issues with Opposing Viewpoints books aim to open readers' minds to the critically divergent views that comprise our world's most important debates.

Introducing Issues with Opposing Viewpoints simplifies for students the enormous and often overwhelming mass of material now available via print and electronic media. Collected in every volume is an array of opinions that captures the essence of a particular controversy or topic. Introducing Issues with Opposing Viewpoints books embody the spirit of nineteenth-century journalist Charles A. Dana's axiom: "Fight for your opinions, but do not believe that they contain the whole truth, or the only truth." Absorbing such contrasting opinions teaches students to analyze the strength of an argument and compare it to its opposition. From this process readers can inform and strengthen their own opinions, or be exposed to new information that will change their minds. Introducing Issues with Opposing Viewpoints is a mosaic of different voices. The authors are statesmen, pundits, academics, journalists, corporations, and ordinary people who have felt compelled to share their experiences and ideas in a public forum. Their words have been collected from newspapers, journals, books, speeches, interviews, and the Internet, the fastest growing body of opinionated material in the world.

Introducing Issues with Opposing Viewpoints shares many of the well-known features of its critically acclaimed parent series, Opposing Viewpoints. The articles are presented in a pro/con format, allowing readers to absorb divergent perspectives side by side. Active reading questions preface each viewpoint, requiring the student to approach the material thoughtfully and carefully. Useful charts, graphs, and cartoons supplement each article. A thorough introduction provides readers with crucial background on an issue. An annotated bibliography points the reader toward articles, books, and Web sites that contain additional information on the topic. An appendix of organizations to contact contains a wide variety of charities, nonprofit organizations, political groups, and private enterprises that each hold a position on the issue at hand. Finally, a comprehensive index allows readers to locate content quickly and efficiently.

Introducing Issues with Opposing Viewpoints is also significantly different from Opposing Viewpoints. As the series title implies, its presentation will help introduce students to the concept of opposing viewpoints, and learn to use this material to aid in critical writing and debate. The series' four-color, accessible format makes the books attractive and inviting to readers of all levels. In addition, each viewpoint has been carefully edited to maximize a reader's understanding of the content. Short but thorough viewpoints capture the essence of an argument. A substantial, thought-provoking essay question placed at the end of each viewpoint asks the student to further investigate the issues raised in the viewpoint, compare and contrast two authors' arguments, or consider how one might go about forming an opinion on the topic at hand. Each viewpoint contains sidebars that include at-a-glance information and handy statistics. A Facts About section located in the back of the book further supplies students with relevant facts and figures.

Following in the tradition of the Opposing Viewpoints series, Greenhaven Press continues to provide readers with invaluable exposure to the controversial issues that shape our world. As John Stuart Mill once wrote: "The only way in which a human being can make some approach to knowing the whole of a subject is by hearing what can be said about it by persons of every variety of opinion and studying all modes in which it can be looked at by every character of mind. No wise man ever acquired his wisdom in any mode but this." It is to this principle that Introducing Issues with Opposing Viewpoints books are dedicated.

Introduction

"If one crazed amateur can violate the airspace of what is supposed to be the most secure building in America and leave his plane piled up a few feet below the President's bedroom, a dedicated terrorist can manage a successful airborne biochemical attack of any major city in the country."

—Michael Reynolds, analyst for the Southern Poverty Law Center's Intelligence Project

The terrorist attacks of September 11, 2001, terrified the nation in a shocking and visceral way. When four planes were hijacked and exploded in the World Trade Center, the Pentagon, and a field in Pennsylvania, images of the devastation circulated the globe, inspiring fear in citizens of all nations. A month later, another insidious terrorist attack was carried out in the United States—yet this one occurred without dramatic photographs and heart-racing video footage. In 2001 a silent, slow, yet deadly act of terror was executed when four letters containing the biological agent anthrax were mailed in the United States. Twenty-three people were infected, five were killed, and countless Americans warily regarded the contents of their mailboxes. A U.S. Senate office building and several post offices were also closed in the ensuing chaos.

The 2001 anthrax attacks made officials realize that a terrorist attack against the United States might not be announced with fireballs and explosions, but could come in the form of a silent yet deadly attack delivered by biological and chemical weapons of mass destruction (WMDs). It was feared that if executed correctly, such an attack could cause damage on an unimaginable scale. But how likely is it that terrorists could actually carry one out? Though no one challenges the idea that WMD attacks are scary, experts often debate whether biological and chemical weapons pose a real threat to the American public.

Some experts believe that it is only a matter of time before the United States sees a large-scale WMD attack on its soil. They reason that with the exception of nuclear bombs, ingredients for biological, chemical, and radiological weapons are relatively inexpensive and portable. Because germs are naturally occurring organisms, they represent a cheap weapon with which terrorists could inflict widespread casualties. Analysts also worry that the raw materials for such weapons are alarmingly easy for terrorists or rogue governments to obtain. In fact, a 2001 Department of Defense report concluded, "Any nation with the political will and a minimal industrial base could produce chemical and biological weapon agents suitable for use."

Biological agents are one example of a WMD that terrorists or rogue governments might choose to use. Biological agents make simple and potentially disastrous weapons. They are made by concentrating large amounts of deadly germs or viruses, and then releasing them in public places. Among the most serious biological agents that can be weaponized are the microorganisms that cause anthrax, botulism, plague, smallpox, and hemorrhagic fever viruses. The release of biological weapons would be at first unnoticed because the germs are not visible to the naked eye and are difficult to detect without proper equipment. Large numbers of Americans could become infected and spread the germs to others before anyone realized that an attack had been undertaken.

Anthrax is an example of a biological agent that could be easily harvested or found in nature by terrorists. It is found in wild and domesticated animals such as cattle, sheep, and goats. Anthrax is common in agricultural regions in less-developed countries, the sorts of areas that can become breeding grounds for terrorist groups. Spores of anthrax could be collected, ground up into a fine powder, and used as a very deadly weapon. This type of attack is often carried out by placing anthrax powder in letters and packages. Several U.S. post offices have experienced anthrax exposures in recent years.

Like bioweapons, chemical weapons could pose a grave threat to Americans if used in a terrorist attack. Toxic chemicals are also inexpensive, readily available, easy to disperse, and can cause agony and death. To understand the devastation such an attack could cause, experts point to the industrial accident that occurred in Bhopal, India, in 1984 when a pesticide plant accidentally released a chemical called methyl isocyanate into the atmosphere. The disaster killed nearly four thousand people. A terrorist attack using such a chemical or on a chemical facility could achieve a similar level of devastation.

But once terrorists had fashioned a biological or chemical WMD, how easy would it be to use in an attack? There is much debate over whether such weapons could actually devastate on the large scale they are feared to be able to. Some believe that with as little as a crop duster (a plane used to spray pesticides on crops), terrorists could spread vast amounts of biochemical weapons over a large area, killing thousands. Yet others argue that biochemical weapons, though deadly, are in fact quite difficult to disperse properly. Many such weapons lose their potency when exposed to air, light, or moisture, and for this reason are actually quite difficult to turn into successful weapons. Therefore, although the U.S. Army and the CIA have estimated that a biochemical attack on the New York City subway system could infect an estimated 3 million people, slight changes in wind, temperature, or weather could render the whole effort a failure.

Although the U.S. military uncovered evidence in Afghanistan that Osama bin Laden's group, Al Qaeda, was researching chemical weapons, experts say that it would also be very difficult for terrorists, working in a makeshift lab, to fabricate an effective chemical weapon. Instead, they believe it would be far more likely for terrorists to turn America's chemical infrastructures into weapons—blowing up a chemical plant or a truck carrying hazardous chemicals, for example, would disperse harmful materials into the air that would have the same effect. A U.S. Army study, for example, estimated that nearly 2.5 million people could die if terrorists were successful in blowing up a chemical plant. But even this type of attack would be difficult to pull off. Since September 11, such sites are heavily guarded, and it is unclear whether terrorists would be able to sneak such a large weapon into the country or get it close enough to a facility to do any real damage.

Researcher Jim Walsch of the Belfer Center for Science and International Affairs at Harvard University calms fears about a biological or chemical WMD attack by pointing out that although chemical and biological weapons have existed since World War I, they have rarely been used. Furthermore, the risk incurred by terrorists or rogue governments who might use biological or chemical weapons might adequately deter them. "No country," states Walsch, "would attack the U.S. with such weapons for fear of nuclear retaliation." Walsch regards attacks such as the 1995 Aum Shinrikyo attack on a Japanese subway one as "more failure than success; 12 people were killed. . . . Had they used a traditional high explosive, the death toll would have been far greater. Many warned that Aum's attack would set off a wave of chemical attacks. That didn't happen."

Examining the likelihood of a biological or chemical attack against the United States is one of many issues explored in *Introducing Issues with Opposing Viewpoints: Weapons of Mass Destruction.* Readers will learn about the key threats posed by WMDs, how WMD proliferation can be prevented, and how rogue nations who seek WMDs should be handled.

Chapter 1

Do Weapons of Mass Destruction Pose a Serious Threat?

Al-Samoud 2 missiles sit in an Iraqi trailer. The United Nations ordered their destruction under UN resolutions imposed after the Gulf War.

The U.S. Is Likely to Be Attacked with Weapons of Mass Destruction

"If terrorists are able to acquire a particularly destructive weapon, they are likely to use it."

Harold Kennedy

In the following viewpoint, author Harold Kennedy presents military opinions that some terrorist groups are willing and determined to carry out biological, chemical, or nuclear terrorist attacks within the United States. Especially troubling is the possibility of an attack with a "dirty bomb," a weapon that is a mixture of conventional explosives with radioactive material. The radioactive elements needed to produce such a device exist in almost every country, and a number of agencies are taking active steps to secure and control their use. Although the terrorist group Al Qaeda has not yet been able to acquire and use such a weapon, it is a very real possibility that the United States must acknowledge and plan for.

Harold Kennedy is a reporter for *National Defense* magazine.

Harold Kennedy, "Counter Terrorism: At Special Ops Forum, Experts Weigh Prospect of WMD Attacks," *National Defense*, vol. 90, March 2006, pp. 40-44. Copyright 2006 National Defense Industrial Association. Reproduced by permission.

1. What potentially dangerous materials did U.S. and coalition troops find stockpiled in Fallujah, Iraq, as reported by Kennedy?
2. According to Kennedy, what type of WMD did Britain and Germany use during World War I?
3. What examples of high-risk radiological materials that could potentially be used to make a dirty bomb does Kennedy list?

A s military leaders devote increasing attention to neutralizing roadside bombs in Iraq, specialists caution that it would be a mistake to dismiss the threat posed by weapons of mass destruction [WMD].

These experts contend that terrorists are bent on using WMD against civilian populations in the United States and allied nations.

Don't Let Guard Down

Many Americans have let down their guard after U.S. and coalition forces in Iraq failed to uncover WMD—which include chemical, biological, radiological and nuclear explosive devices—experts told a 2006 conference in Tampa, Fla., sponsored by the U.S. Special Operations Command, or SOCOM.

Instead, they noted, the Defense Department is focusing now on defeating improvised explosive devices [IED], the handmade conventional bombs that have been taking a heavy toll among U.S. and coalition service personnel and civilians in Iraq.

Officials at the special operations conference acknowledged the importance of the counter-IED project, but they warned military leaders not to downplay the threats posed by the possibility of a chemical, biological, radiological or nuclear weapon falling into the hands of terrorists.

The devastation from such a weapon detonated in a major city would dwarf the impact of any single conventional IED, said Army Lt. Col. John Campbell, the chief of SOCOM's chemical, biological, radiological and nuclear branch. And if terrorists are able to acquire a particularly destructive weapon, they are likely to use it, he said. "The threat is real, and we have to be prepared for it," he said.

The United States needs to plan for every contingency and be willing to adapt to the unexpected, Campbell said. "Events like Hurricane Katrina show that the best plans don't always work, and we have to be ready for that."

Keeping Up the Pressure

More than four years after the 9/11 attacks, Osama Bin Laden "hasn't resorted yet to [WMD]," Campbell said. "Why not?

"My personal opinion is that we have been chasing him so hard, he hasn't had the opportunity," he said. "We need to keep up the pressure."

While U.S. and coalition troops did not uncover large stores of WMD in Iraq, they did find evidence that insurgent forces have been trying to develop unconventional weapons, said Army Brig. Gen. Stephen V. Reeves, the Defense Department's joint program executive officer for chemical and biological defense. "In Fallujah, we found a chemical lab with stockpiles of potassium cyanide and sodium cyanide," he told conferees.

Both are potentially fatal to anybody exposed to them and can be used to make a chemical bomb, Reeves said. Those devices "are remarkably simple to make and reasonably effective to use," he said.

While Al Qaeda so far hasn't been able to acquire and use such weapons, others have. During World War I, both Germany and Britain used poison gas on the battlefield.

In the 1980s, Saddam Hussein employed it against enemy troops in the Iran-Iraq war, and reportedly even against his own rebellious Kurdish civilians. In 1995, the Aum Shinrikyo cult released the deadly nerve agent, sarin, into the Tokyo subway system. In 2001, somebody mailed letters containing deadly anthrax bacteria to several news media offices and two U.S. senators. That case remains unsolved.

Many terrorist organizations wouldn't use WMD if they got their hands on them, because doing so would undermine popular support for their cause, said Robert E. Neumann, who manages the EAI Corporation's support program for SOCOM. "If the [Irish Republican Army] got a nuclear bomb, I'm sure they would turn it in," he said. "Using it would not be in their interest."

On the other hand, if Al Qaeda got such a bomb, "I'm absolutely convinced that they would find a symbolic target and hit it," Neumann

Biological weapons expert Dr. William Patrick demonstrates how easy it is to launch biological agents into the air.

said. "All of their targets—the World Trade Center, the Pentagon, the London subway system—have had a symbolic value. They want to send a message to themselves, their supporters and their god."

A nuclear bomb, however, may be too difficult for organizations such as Al Qaeda to acquire, Campbell said. "I think they'll take the easy way out," be said.

"One of the biggest fears I have is that they'll develop a chemical IED," Campbell said. "We all know Saddam had chemical weapons. We have people in this room who have seen them.

"If you strap a piece of dynamite to an old, Soviet-era chemical warhead, which we have found in Iraq, you can have a profound psychological impact."

The casualties from such an attack need not be high for the operation to succeed, Campbell said. He noted that five people died in the 2001 anthrax attacks and that 12 perished in the Tokyo sarin incident.

The terrorists "want to scare people," Campbell said. "The crux of terrorism is to destroy their enemy's morale. And there is something inherently evil about WMD that really frightens people."

George Thompson, president of Chemical Compliance Systems Inc., of Lake Hopatcong, N.J., agreed. "You can imagine if they blow up one of our high schools," he said. "How many parents would send their kids to school the next day?"

The "Dirty Bomb" Threat

One weapon designed to cause panic is the so-called dirty bomb, said Kurt Westerman, a manager for the National Nuclear Security Administration's Office of Global Radiological Threat Reduction. A dirty bomb is one that combines a conventional explosive, such as dynamite, with radioactive material.

FAST FACT

According to an AP-Ipsos poll taken in September 2005, 53 percent of Americans think a nuclear attack by terrorists is somewhat likely to occur within the United States.

If such a device were detonated, officials said, it would kill only a small number of people, but it could contaminate several city blocks, spreading fear at least initially and requiring a costly cleanup.

What worries Westerman's agency—which is an arm of the U.S. Energy Department—is that the radioactive elements needed for a dirty bomb are widespread. "High-risk radiological materials exist in virtually every country," he said. "There are thousands in the United States alone." Such materials, ranging from pocket-size to truck-size, are used at hospitals, research facilities, and industrial and construction sites. Examples include medical pacemakers, nuclear-powered gauge and calibration tools, and radioisotope thermoelectric generators.

"These materials are not adequately secured, and that poses an immediate and urgent proliferation and terrorist threat," Westerman warned.

The job of preventing terrorists from getting their hands on such materials has been assigned to a number of U.S. military units and federal agencies.

In 2003, Defense Secretary Donald Rumsfeld ordered the Special Operations Command to take the military lead in the global war on terrorism. "We're the pointy end of the spear," said Army Lt. Gen. Dell L. Daily, director of SOCOM's Center for Special Operations, which coordinates the command's efforts with other U.S. and allied military units and agencies.

One SOCOM assignment is to find and seize terrorist WMD devices, laboratories and factories where they may be made, and training facilities where terrorists learn to use them.

The command has had little to say about its operations. However, it has been reported widely that special-operations units led the fruitless searches for WMD in Iraq and Afghanistan. They also have participated in an ongoing series of maritime-interdiction exercises around the world, where U.S. and allied naval forces train to board and seize merchant ships suspected of transporting WMD-related materials.

The Energy Department has been working since 1993 to improve international controls of nuclear and radiological material, Westerman said. In 2004, the department consolidated its efforts into a single organization, the Office of Radiological Threat Reduction, which has initiated programs in 40 countries. Within the United States alone, more than 11,000 sealed radiological devices have been recovered. Worldwide, more than 500,000 of such devices are not properly secured, Westerman said. "People tell us you'll never recover them all, and that's true. But if we leave the easy fruit out there, the bad guys will get it, and we'll never know it until it's too late."

EVALUATING THE AUTHORS' ARGUMENTS:

In this viewpoint, Harold Kennedy provides numerous examples of defense and military personnel who argue the United States is increasingly at risk for a WMD attack. In the following viewpoint, William M. Arkin argues that since September 11, 2001, the U.S. is increasingly safe from a WMD attack. After reading both viewpoints, with which auther do you agree? Explain your answer.

The U.S. Is Not Likely to Be Attacked with Weapons of Mass Destruction

William M. Arkin

"The threat of nuclear, biological, or chemical war has diminished to a lower level than at anytime in most of our lifetimes."

In the following viewpoint author William M. Arkin argues that the threat of a weapon of mass destruction (WMD) attack against the United States has been blown out of proportion. Over the past thirty years, he says, fewer nations have WMDs, and more nations are subject to anti-WMD treaties and monitoring agreements. The threat of a WMD attack has been especially low since September 11, 2001, he claims, because more nations have become vigilant against WMDs falling into the wrong hands. Because the idea of a WMD attack is so scary, Arkin says that politicians play upon this fear to push their own agendas. The world is safer than Americans think, and Arkin concludes that the chance of terrorists carrying out a WMD attack is unlikely.

William M. Arkin is an online columnist for the *Washington Post* and a military analyst for NBC News. His work has been published in the *Bulletin of the Atomic Scientists*, from which this viewpoint was taken.

AS YOU READ, CONSIDER THE FOLLOWING QUESTIONS:
1. How much have world stockpiles of weapons of mass destruction decreased since the late-1960s Cold War peak, according to Arkin?
2. What are five nations that have gotten "out of the WMD business," as reported by Arkin?
3. What pattern does Arkin think the United States is repeating in Iran?

Conventional wisdom says that the wide availability of fissile materials and nuclear know-how make the likelihood of nuclear use by a terrorist group some time in the future extremely high. From Vice President Dick Cheney to Massachusetts Democratic Senator Ted Kennedy, there is near unanimity about this threat of nuclear terrorism. Virtually every government agrees; so do most experts in the arms control community, the scientific establishment, academia, the news media, and even the peace movement. . . .

On this fifth anniversary of 9/11, with Iraq out of the WMD business and Al Qaeda on the run and denied state sanctuary, one might think that the concern and panic about nuclear terrorism would have diminished, if not disappeared. To many though, the World Trade Center and Pentagon attacks merely confirmed a decades-old presumption that if they could, terrorists would acquire weapons of mass destruction, and they would also use

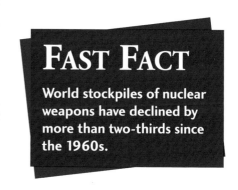

FAST FACT

World stockpiles of nuclear weapons have declined by more than two-thirds since the 1960s.

them. This threat is not only amorphous, in that it cannot be measured in warheads or forces and cannot be "deterred" in the traditional sense. It is also based on faith and completely divorced from intent, political realities, and technological possibilities. But because the consequences of failure are so high, it is a threat that never really goes away.

Could terrorists really obtain sufficient materials and put together all of what would be needed to manufacture a nuclear weapon? I'll go out on a limb and say, not after 9/11.

Letting Fear Take Control

Anxiety about nuclear terrorism predates the events of 9/11. It goes back at least to the early 1970s when European terrorism was rampant and nuclear weapons were stored at more than 1,000 depots worldwide, a high percentage of them in western Europe. Since then, concern about nuclear terrorism has ebbed and flowed with the times and been employed by counterterrorism and security types, by arms control and nonproliferation specialists and activists, and by antinuclear power advocates. The joining of proliferation and counterterrorism concerns in the 1990s—with the specter of a WMD terrorist attack—proved a particularly potent and enduring combination.

Today, government officials and analysts, even the communities that one might expect to express deep skepticism in the aftermath of the Iraq experience, enlist nuclear terrorism and tout it as the great fear. The recent Weapons of Mass Destruction Commission couldn't resist including terror in the title of its final report earlier this year [in 2006], placing counterterrorism on equal ground with disarmament and nonproliferation. The threat, the commission said, demanded improvements in security and greater control of nuclear materials as well as a return to general arms control and disarmament negotiations.

No Evidence of a Nuclear Threat

There is no factual answer as to whether the threat of nuclear terrorism is actually worthy of equal billing. . . .

[In March 2006], Director of National Intelligence John Negroponte and the director of the Defense Intelligence Agency, Lieutenant General Michael Maples, testified before Congress that the threat of terrorist

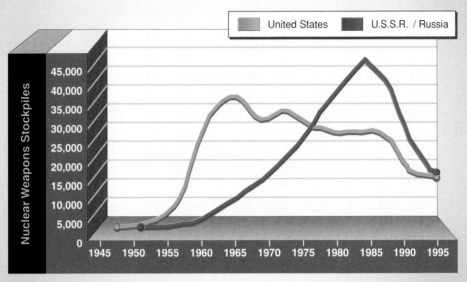

U.S. and U.S.S.R. Nuclear Stockpiles

United States ■ U.S.S.R. / Russia

Nuclear Weapons Stockpiles

45,000
40,000
35,000
30,000
25,000
20,000
15,000
10,000
5,000
0

1945 1950 1955 1960 1965 1970 1975 1980 1985 1990 1995

Source: http://en.wikipedia.org/wiki/Image:US_and_USSR_nuclear_stockpiles.png.

attack with WMD was "more likely" than an attack by any state, including Iran and North Korea. Negroponte reported, "In fact, intelligence reporting indicates that nearly forty terrorist organizations, insurgencies, or cults have used, possessed, or expressed an interest in chemical, biological, radiological, or nuclear agents or weapons. Many are capable of conducting simple, small-scale attacks, such as poisonings, or using improvised chemical devices." Maples added, "Al Qaeda's stated intention to conduct an attack exceeding the destruction of 9/11 raises the possibility that future attacks may involve unconventional weapons."

Neither Negroponte nor Maples offered any detail indicating evidence or even trends toward terrorists acquiring any of these capabilities. Instead, they put forth the "possibility" of a future terrorist WMD attack, thus promoting the war on terrorism while seeking bureaucratic sanctuary in an enduring state of national insecurity. A few months before the 2004 election and less than a week before the third anniversary of 9/11, Vice President Cheney similarly demonstrated the political utility of this conceit, saying that if the United States made the wrong choice on November 2 "then the danger is that we'll get hit again." . . .

The WMD Threat Has Been Drastically Reduced

Is there a possibility that there is a different "truth?" In the world I see after thirty years in this business, the United States and Russia have withdrawn thousands of nuclear weapons from service; nations have denuclearized aircraft and naval ships; and they have lessened high operational–readiness levels. In this world, the spread of nuclear weapons—particularly U.S. and Russian nuclear weapons, which were once deployed in scores of countries at many hundreds of sites—has significantly declined. Britain and France have significantly reduced their arsenals; China's arsenal has pretty much stood still. Worldwide stockpiles of nuclear weapons have declined by more than two-thirds since the late-1960's Cold War peak.

In this world, the roster of countries out of the WMD business far exceeds the numbers who have gone nuclear in the past thirty years: Iraq, Libya, South Africa, Brazil, and Argentina, not to name the list of northern democracies, from Japan to Sweden. Former Soviet republics agreed to relinquish physical possession of former Soviet weapons. Nuclear-weapon-free zones now exist in Latin America, the South Pacific, Africa, and Southeast Asia. International bodies are experienced and unsentimental in pursuit of the craft of inspections and disarmament. Like it or not, disarmament by force in Iraq has also communicated to potential state proliferators the cost of defying the international community. Post-Iraq, moreover, there is ever-greater vigilance in both monitoring and interdicting the trade in nuclear materials.

All of the evidence indicates that the threat of nuclear, biological, or chemical war has diminished to a lower level than at anytime in most of our lifetimes, yet the specter of a "nuclear handoff" from a nuclear nation to a terrorist group or the supposed ready availability of nuclear materials drives a completely different supposition. This cataclysmic picture has no factual rebuttal, yet that does not mean that nuclear terrorism is a vital, valid, or, even, the most important WMD threat. . . .

Finding Nuclear Threats Where We Create Them

In the run up to the 2003 Iraq War, as the Bush administration mobilized public opinion and prepared physically for war, there was an expert debate. Prague, mobile laboratories, aluminum tubes, ranges of missiles—Washington debated capabilities, as well as its own prospective war plans, the best targets, and how many troops were needed. By sheer repetition, Iraqi WMD materialized. The infinite nature of the threat promoted and produced only one answer: war. The only real question was what color it was going to be.

Are we just repeating this pattern when it comes to Iran? There are centrifuges instead of aluminum tubes, Hezbollah instead of Al Qaeda. Again, "intelligence" about intentions and capabilities, U.N. inspections, and the involvement and consent of the international community, dominate the discussion. WMD experts, all of whom sound eminently reasonable and who eschew the language of extremism, ask whether the intelligence is good enough, what the targets might be, whether U.S. forces are sufficient to do the job. They simultaneously jump on every nuclear twitch, subsist on each nuclear breath. The

Some believe the threat of WMDs is slim, since many nuclear powers are subject to treaties and inspections as well as the destruction of potential weapons and components.

argument suggests that if there is sufficient intelligence, if the targets are found, if US forces are mustered and a sound war plan developed, and if the international community gets thwarted, then another pre-emptive war is not only inevitable but necessary.

Iran may be a decade or more away from producing a nuclear weapon, an endeavor and a timetable made all the more difficult if not impossible by the post-9/11 realities and the vigilance and competence of the nonproliferation industry. Theirs is God's work. Treaties, inspections, and regimes of control have worked.

A more accurate picture of the state of WMD five years after 9/11 is that the threat has indeed diminished. A truer intelligence assessment is that the danger has steadily declined despite the continued existence of eight nuclear nations and two serious rogues. To argue in favor of a new perspective on WMD is not cockeyed optimism or naiveté. But to get there will require breaking the near-unanimous stranglehold of the Cheney and Kennedy camps. Theirs is the real nuclear terror.

EVALUATING THE AUTHORS' ARGUMENTS:

In this viewpoint William M. Arkin argues politicians such as Dick Cheney have no evidence to back up claims that terrorists intend to use weapons of mass destruction against Americans. How do you think Harold Kennedy, author of the previous viewpoint, would respond to this argument?

Iraq Possessed Weapons of Mass Destruction

Rick Santorum and Peter Hoekstra

"Weapons have been discovered; more weapons exist."

In the following viewpoint Senator Rick Santorum and Congressman Peter Hoekstra claim that Iraq possessed weapons of mass destruction (WMDs) prior to being invaded by the United States in 2003. They discuss the findings of a 2006 intelligence document that reports on stocks of chemical weapons munitions found within the country. Because the war in Iraq was undertaken due to a belief that former dictator Saddam Hussein possessed WMDs, Santorum and Hoekstra argue the war was justified. Santorum and Hoekstra also argue that more WMDs exist in Iraq. They therefore advise the United States to stay the course in Iraq so that unrecovered WMDs do not fall into the hands of terrorists.

Rick Santorum is a Republican senator from Pennsylvania. He is known for supporting conservative values and the war in Iraq. Peter Hoekstra is a Republican congressman from Michigan.

Rick Santorum and Peter Hoekstra, "News Conference to Release a Report on Iraqi Weapons of Mass Destruction." www.ricksantorum.com/News/Read.ASPX?ID=1370, June 21, 2006.

Good afternoon. Senator Rick Santorum. With me, Chairman of the House Intelligence Committee Pete Hoekstra. Today we are here to make public a document, an unclassified version of a document that Congressman Hoekstra and I have been working on, trying to uncover, I guess, or find out about with respect to weapons of mass destruction, particularly chemical weapons recovered in Iraq.

Proving Doubters Wrong

On the floor of the Senate today we are debating the issue of the war in Iraq, and three of my colleagues just today said the following things.

Jack Reed, quote: "We've heard the initial defenses of the approach to Iraq as we were going after weapons of mass destruction. There were none. They were not there."

Chris Dodd: "Mr. President, that if I had known then what I know now, namely that Saddam Hussein possessed no weapons of mass destruction, I would not have given the president my vote."

Patty Murray: "We looked for weapons of mass destruction and we found none."

Congressman Hoekstra and I are here today to say that we have found weapons of mass destruction in Iraq, chemical weapons. It's a document that was developed by our intelligence community which for the last two and a half months I have been pursuing. . . .

The unclassified version of this report states as follows. Quote: Since 2003, coalition forces have recovered approximately 500 weapons munitions which contain degraded mustard or sarin nerve agent. Despite many efforts to locate and destroy Iraq's pre-Gulf War chemical munitions, filled and unfilled pre-Gulf War chemical munitions are assessed to still exist. . . .

That means that in addition to the 500 there are filled and unfilled munitions still believed to exist within the country.

WMDs Exist in Iraq

Pre-Gulf War Iraqi chemical weapons could be sold on the black market. Use of these weapons by terrorists or insurgent groups would have implications for coalition forces in Iraq. The possibility of use outside of Iraq cannot be ruled out. The most likely munitions remaining are sarin- and mustard-filled projectiles.

And I underscored filled. The purity of the agents inside the munitions depends on many factors, including the manufacturing process, potential additives and environmental storage conditions. While agents degrade over time, chemical warfare agents remain hazardous and potentially lethal.

It has been reported in the open press that insurgents and Iraqi groups desire to acquire and use chemical weapons.

Workers seal leaks in Iraqi rockets believed to be filled with sarin, a chemical nerve agent.

Toxic Weapons: How They Kill

There are many biological and chemical agents that can be weaponized. Each varies in its symptoms and effects on the body.

BIOLOGICAL TOXINS

Toxin	Symptoms	Effects if untreated
Aflatoxin	Headache, jaundice, gastrointestinal distress	Liver disease, internal bleeding, possible death
Anthrax	Fever, malaise, cough, respiratory distress	Shock and death within 36 hours of severe symptoms
Botulinum toxins	Weakness, dizziness, dry throat, blurred vision, problems speaking and hearing, difficulty swallowing	Paralysis, respiratory failure, death
Bubonic plague	Malaise, high fever, tender lymph nodes	Blood poisoning, death
Cholera	Vomiting, abdominal distension, pain, diarrhea	Severe dehydration, shock, death
Pneumonic plague	High fever, chills, headache, coughing up blood, blood poisoning	Respiratory failure, circulatory collapse, heavy bleeding, death
Q fever	Fever, cough, chest pain	Generally not fatal
Ricin	Weakness, fever, cough, hypothermia	Dangerously low blood pressure, heart failure, death
Smallpox	Malaise, fever, vomiting, headache, backache, blister-like rash	Bone marrow depression, bleeding, death
Staphylococcal enterotoxin B	Fever, chills, headache, muscle aches, cough	Septic shock, death
Tularemia	Swollen glands, fever, headache, malaise, weight loss, nonproductive cough	Generally not fatal
Viral hemorrhagic fevers	Easy bleeding, red spots on skin, low blood pressure, flushed face and chest, swelling of ankles and other joints	Uncontrollable bleeding, circulatory collapse, death

CHEMICAL TOXINS

Toxin	Symptoms	Effects if untreated
Nerve agents, including VX, GB, and GD	Runny nose, tightness of chest, dim vision, pinpointing of eye pupils, difficulty breathing, drooling, excessive sweating, nausea, vomiting, cramps, involuntary urination and defecation, jerking, staggering, headache, confusion, drowsiness	Convulsions, coma, cessation of breathing, death
Sulfur Mustard Agent	Eye irritation, skin blemishes and blisters, inflammation of the nose, throat and lung, malaise, vomiting, fever. Classified as a carcinogen.	Blocks cell growth, suppresses bone marrow

Sources: U.S. Army Medical Research Institute of Infectious Diseases.
U.S. Army Center for Health Promotion and Preventive Medicine.

This is an incredibly—in my mind—significant finding. The idea that, as my colleagues have repeatedly said in this debate on the other side of the aisle, that there are no weapons of mass destruction, is in fact false.

We have found over 500 weapons of mass destruction. And in fact have found that there are additional weapons of mass destruction—chemical weapons, still in the country, that need to be recovered.

And so, I would suggest that this is a very important look-back. We've been focused and continue to focus on what we need to do moving forward, but it is important for the American public to understand that these weapons did in fact exist, were present in the country, and were in fact and continue to be a threat to us. . . .

The War in Iraq Was Justified

I think it's important to put this report in the context of the WMD discussion. Everyone knows, and has agreed, that there was WMD in Iraq prior to the Gulf War, the first Gulf War. He [Saddam Hussein] used weapons of mass destruction extensively, killing thousands of his own people and thousands of Iranians.

From the Kay report and the Duelfer report [prewar reports on Iraq's WMDs], the conclusions that they reached indicated that during that period of time from the Gulf War to Operation Iraqi Freedom, there was evidence of continuing research and development of WMD, an ongoing effort with various kinds of chemicals, research programs and those types of things.

The piece that still remains unanswered, or remained unanswered, was that piece of exactly what, other than the programs, what existed in Iraq in 2003?

The Iraqi Survey Group, or the impression that the Iraqi Survey Group left with the American people was they didn't find anything.

The report that Rick and I reference . . . says: Weapons have

FAST FACT

In 1988 former Iraqi dictator Saddam Hussein dropped bombs containing mustard gas, sarin nerve gas, and tabun gas on the Kurdish city of Halabja. As many as 3,200 to 5,000 people were killed, and many survivors suffered long-term health problems.

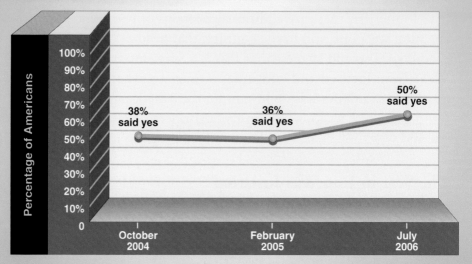

Americans Continue to Believe Iraq Possessed Weapons of Mass Destruction

According to a July 2006 poll, Americans increasingly believe weapons of mass destruction were found in Iraq. The poll asked Americans whether or not they believe Iraq had weapons of mass destruction when the United States invaded.

Percentage of Americans

100%
90%
80%
70%
60%
50%
40%
30%
20%
10%
0

38% said yes

36% said yes

50% said yes

October 2004   February 2005   July 2006

Source: The Harris Poll® #57, "Belief that Iraq Had Weapons of Mass Destruction Has Increased Substantially," July 21, 2006.

been discovered; more weapons exist. And they state that Iraq was not a WMD-free zone, that there are continuing threats from the materials that are or may still be in Iraq. . . .

And since that period of time, we have found hundreds. This assessment says more exist. And I think what that points out is that there's still a lot about Iraq that we don't fully understand. . . .

The Next Steps

So what do we do after this report comes out?

Number one, I think Rick and I are in agreement: More of the classified report has to be released to the American public. They need to get this in a more complete context.

The second thing that needs to happen is under the direction of the House Intelligence Committee, we are going to do and go back and ask for a more complete reporting by the various intelligence agencies as to reporting on WMD. . . .

Finding these quantities of weapons indicates that they're out there. The terrorists have indicated in press reports that they desire to acquire and use chemical weapons.

So the question is: Have we secured all the sites? What efforts are we taking, right now, to secure, identify and locate all of these sites so that we locate them and find them and move forward before they get into the hands of people who we'd prefer not to have access to them?

EVALUATING THE AUTHORS' ARGUMENTS:

Rick Santorum and Peter Hoekstra begin their statement by quoting from opponents who believe there were no weapons of mass destruction in Iraq. Why do you think they did this? What did it add to the tone of their essay? Did you find this technique effective in proving their point? Explain your answer.

Iraq Did Not Possess Weapons of Mass Destruction

Alan Reynolds

In the following viewpoint author Alan Reynolds challenges claims made by Senator Rick Santorum and Congressman Peter Hoekstra that Iraq possessed weapons of mass destruction. Reynolds acknowledges that a few hundred artillery shells filled with chemical weapons were found, but argues that such weapons pose little danger and do not qualify as threatening weapons of mass destruction. For one, Reynolds claims, the artillery shells are too big and cumbersome to be used by terrorists for any type of attack. Secondly, he argues, the chemicals they are filled with are old and not likely potent. He argues that terrorists will have little use for such weapons if they ever get their hands on them. Reynolds concludes that such discoveries do not justify the war in Iraq, which was undertaken to rid Iraq of weapons of mass destruction that posed a serious threat to the United States.

"Heavy artillery shells are battlefield weapons— not something easily hidden in terrorist suitcases."

Alan Reynolds, "No Intelligence (Still)," *Washington Times*, July 9, 2006. Reproduced by permission of Alan Reynolds and Creators Syndicate.

Alan Reynolds is a senior fellow with the Cato Institute, a nonprofit public policy research foundation headquartered in Washington, D.C. His columns are nationally syndicated in newspapers and magazines such as the *Washington Times*, where this article appeared.

AS YOU READ, CONSIDER THE FOLLOWING QUESTIONS:
1. How many terrorist-caused deaths have there been from sarin gas attacks, according to Reynolds?
2. What does Reynolds say is the one possible strategic value of Iraq's outdated artillery shells?
3. What threat is posed from sulfur mustard, or mustard gas, as described by Reynolds?

Some of my favorite conservative commentators appear dismayed that the White House and press paid little attention to news that "Coalition forces have recovered approximately 500 weapons munitions (in Iraq) which contain degraded mustard or sarin nerve agent."

That item came from a one-page memo by John D. Negroponte, director of national intelligence, sent to placate Michigan Rep. Peter Hoekstra, chairman of the House intelligence committee. Pennsylvania Sen. Rick Santorum also got involved. Along with many Republican enthusiasts, they believe the president should stand up and shout: "See, I *told* you so! Saddam really did have weapons of mass destruction!"

L. Brent Bozell, the persuasive president of the Media Research Center, complained that major newspapers buried this story. Yet the media could not possibly have done that if the administration had trumpeted the news. Bozell suspects that "Team Bush" has been silenced "out of intimidation by the media." Not likely.

Weapons Discovery Is Not a Big Deal

First, finding those 500 artillery shells was not much of a surprise. My column last November, "No Intelligence," critiqued the 2002 CIA report about weapons of mass destruction (WMD) in Iraq. Among few concrete facts within that otherwise slippery report, I remarked, was that "Iraq has not accounted for . . . about 550 artillery shells filled with mustard agent."

That information came from the vilified U.N. Monitoring, Verification and Inspection Commission (UNMOVIC). I did not doubt such artillery shells might be left over from the 1991 Iraq War. But, I asked, how anyone could "actually imagine that terrorists could simply . . . fire artillery shells from cannons on U.S. streets?"

Heavy artillery shells are battlefield weapons—not something easily hidden in terrorist suitcases. A 155-millimeter shell is over six inches in diameter and requires a cannon about 10 feet to 12 feet long. A mere tank will not suffice to launch such shells. A 155-millimeter German howitzer weighs 55 tons.

Weapons Found Are Minimally Destructive

The Negroponte memo concerns "Iraq's filled and unfilled pre-Gulf war chemical munitions." This refers to "sarin- and mustard-filled projectiles," meaning 155-millimeter artillery shells. "While agents

Senator Carl Levin is among those who expressed concerns about the intelligence sharing that occurred in the time leading up to the war in Iraq.

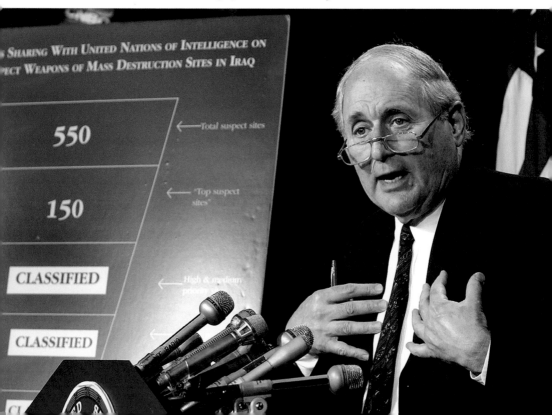

degrade over time," the memo continues, "chemical warfare agents remain hazardous and potentially lethal."

Most chemicals are hazardous waste. But "potentially lethal" could mean anything, including swallowing a pound of the stuff. The nerve gas sarin can certainly be lethal if it is fresh and nearby. Sarin was used in a 1995 terrorist attack on the Tokyo subway system that killed 12 and in a 1994 attack that killed seven in Matsumoto, Japan.

Nineteen deaths are as close to "mass destruction" as the world has seen from terrorist use (as opposed to battlefield use) of chemical or biological agents. Yet sarin degrades very quickly. UNMOVIC concluded years ago that it would be "unlikely that (Iraq's sarin-filled munitions) would still be viable today."

What about the heavy artillery shells filled with old "mustard gas" (sulfur mustard)? That is hazardous waste material, to be sure —anyone who opened those shells without the proper gloves would still be badly blistered. But it is a highly unlikely weapon of mass destruction, particularly in this form at this late date.

Exposure Is "Usually Not Fatal"

In 2000, the Federal Emergency Management Agency reported: "The United States Congress has directed that the U.S. Army destroy certain kinds of chemical weapons stockpiled at eight U.S. Army installations in the continental United States over the next several years. Experts believe the chance of an accident involving these obsolete chemical munitions is remote." The U.S. quietly got rid of its obsolete sulfur mustard by February 2005 without any risk of mass destruction.

Sulfur mustard is commonly called "mustard gas," but it is neither mustard nor a gas. It is liquid at temperatures above 58 degrees Fahrenheit and called "mustard" because of its odor and color. It causes blisters and is potentially harmful to the lungs and eyes (which is why infantry carry gas masks).

According to the Centers for Disease Control: "Exposure to sulfur mustard is usually not fatal. When sulfur mustard was used during World War I, it killed fewer than 5 percent of the people who were exposed and got medical care." Most estimates of lethality range from 1 percent to 3 percent.

Sulfur mustard inside Iraq's old heavy artillery shells was a battlefield weapon. Its strategic value might have been to slow down opposing troops by forcing them to wear protective suits and gas masks in Iraq's extremely hot climate.

Not True Weapons of Mass Destruction

Artillery shells of any sort are not terrorist weapons, but shells filled with conventional explosives are far deadlier than those with sulfur mustard. Any degraded sulfur mustard left inside such shells would be very difficult to remove without destroying the chemical agent (and the person doing the removal).

The reason sulfur mustard was banned by the Geneva Convention in 1925 was not because it was lethal (it is far less lethal than legal explosives), but because blistering caused extreme pain and sometimes blindness.

The concept of antique mustard gas as some awesome new "weapon of mass destruction" appears traceable to an oft-repeated story about Kurdish deaths due to other causes (including sarin). The Council on Foreign Relations Website says: "Saddam Hussein used mustard gas on the Kurds. . . . The worst attack occurred in March 1988 in the Kurdish village of Halabja; a combination of chemical agents including mustard gas and sarin killed 5,000 people." Yet the October 2002 CIA report claimed only "hundreds" of casualties at Halabja and said the intended targets were Iranians.

There Is No Threat from These Weapons

The Negroponte memo purports to be worried that "pre-Gulf war Iraqi chemical weapons could be sold on the black market. Use of these weapons by terrorists or insurgent groups would have implications for Coalition forces in Iraq. The possibility of use outside Iraq cannot be ruled out."

This is the same sort of devious "what if" conjecture that filled the 2002 CIA report. We cannot rule out the possibility that aliens in flying saucers are about to take over the Earth. And we cannot rule out the possibility that unicorns really do exist.

In reality, any "use of these weapons (artillery shells) by terrorists or insurgent groups" would require their possession of 55-ton self-propelled howitzers. Can you imagine finding one of those heavily armed vehicles cruising around unnoticed in Baghdad, much less in New York City? Even if terrorists could fire heavy artillery shells in either city, why would they want them filled with something that causes blisters much more often than death?

The president was judicious to downplay this nonstory about finding a few hundred heavy artillery shells filled with pre-1991 sulfur mustard. To have done otherwise could have proved very embarrassing. His conservative critics would likewise be wise to drop it.

EVALUATING THE AUTHORS' ARGUMENTS:

In this viewpoint Alan Reynolds challenges the claim of Senator Santorum and Congressman Hoekstra that weapons found in Iraq posed any danger to the United States. After reading both viewpoints, what is your opinion of the discovery of artillery shells in Iraq? Do you believe the discovery justified the war in Iraq or not? Explain your answer using evidence from the text.

Chapter 2

How Can the Spread of Weapons of Mass Destruction Be Prevented?

Antiterrorist special unit members conduct a multinational exercise intended to capture weapons of mass destruction at sea.

The Nuclear Non-Proliferation Treaty Can Prevent the Spread of Weapons of Mass Destruction

"The [Nuclear Non-Proliferation Treaty] is a critical tool in the global struggle against pro-liferation."

Stephen G. Rademaker

In the following viewpoint author Stephen G. Rademaker argues that the Nuclear Non-Proliferation Treaty (NPT) is the single most important tool for preventing the spread of weapons of mass destruction (WMDs). The NPT is an international treaty that nations sign promising to abandon nuclear weapons programs and prevent the spread of WMDs. Thanks to the NPT, argues Rademaker, thousands of nuclear weapons and ballistic missiles have been eliminated. Furthermore, through the NPT the international community has persuaded previously rogue nations such as Libya to abandon their nuclear weapons programs. Rademaker concludes that the world must work together to meet

Stephen G. Rademaker, "U.S. Statement at the 2005 Nuclear Non-Proliferation Treaty Review Conference," U.S. Department of State publication, May 2, 2005. U.S. Department of State, Washington, DC.

challenges posed to the NPT so the treaty can continue to thwart the spread of WMDs.

Stephen G. Rademaker is the assistant secretary of state for arms control. He delivered these remarks at the United Nations for the Seventh Review Conference of the Nuclear Non-Proliferation Treaty.

AS YOU READ, CONSIDER THE FOLLOWING QUESTIONS:
1. What five nations does the author say have given up their nuclear programs in exchange for international protection and acceptance?
2. What does UN Resolution 1540 require states to do, as described by the author?
3. What challenges threaten the NPT, according to Rademaker?

The Nuclear Non-Proliferation Treaty (NPT) is a key legal barrier against the spread of nuclear weapons and material related to the production of such weapons. That we can meet today, 35 years after the Treaty entered into force, and not count 20 or more nuclear weapon states—as some predicted in the 1960s—is a sign of the Treaty's success. NPT parties can be justly proud of the NPT's contribution to global security.

Security for All Nations

Nearly 190 states are now party to the Treaty, the greatest number of parties to any multilateral security agreement, save the United Nations Charter. . . .

The NPT is fundamentally a treaty for mutual security. It is clear that the security of all member states depends on unstinting adherence to the Treaty's nonproliferation norms by all other parties. The Treaty's principal beneficiaries are those member states that do *not* possess nuclear weapons because they can be assured that their neighbors also do not possess nuclear weapons. Strict compliance with nonproliferation obligations is essential to regional stability, to forestalling nuclear arms races, and to preventing resources needed for economic development from being squandered in a destabilizing and economically unproductive pursuit of weapons.

Successes and Achievements

There has been important progress in advancing the NPT's objectives. One clear success is the recent Libyan decision to abandon its clandestine nuclear weapons program, a program aided by the A. Q. Khan network. Libya should be commended for making the strategic decision to return to NPT compliance, to voluntarily give up its nuclear weapons program, and to cooperate with the IAEA [International Atomic Energy Agency] and others. In doing so, it moved to end its damaging international isolation and paved the way for improved relations with the international community.

Libya has joined other states, including South Africa, Ukraine, Belarus, and Kazakhstan, that have wisely concluded that their security interests are best served by turning away from nuclear weapons and coming into full compliance with the NPT as non-nuclear weapon states. This demonstrates that, in a world of strong nonproliferation norms, it is never too late to make the decision to become a fully compliant NPT state. In all of these cases, including the most recent case of Libya, such a decision was amply rewarded.

We have also had success in designing new tools outside of the NPT that complement the Treaty. The Proliferation Security Initiative (PSI)

Crates of nuclear weapons and materials were removed from Libya after Libyan president Muammar al-Qaddafi decided to end his nation's weapons of mass destruction program.

is one such important new tool. First proposed by President [George W.] Bush in Krakow, Poland on May 31, 2003, over 60 nations have now associated themselves with this effort against the international outlaws that traffic in deadly materials. We are pleased that the PSI was endorsed by Security Council Resolution 1540 and by the Secretary General's High Level Panel on Threats, Challenges and Change, and we reaffirm our determination not to shrink from using this important new tool.

Challenges Facing the NPT

We cannot simply celebrate these successes, however. While these successes are important, more must be done. Today, the Treaty is facing the most serious challenge in its history due to instances of noncompliance. Although the vast majority of member states have lived up to their NPT nonproliferation obligations that constitute the Treaty's most important contribution to international peace and security, some have not.

Indeed, some continue to use the pretext of a peaceful nuclear program to pursue the goal of developing nuclear weapons. We must confront this challenge in order to ensure that the Treaty remains relevant. This Review Conference provides an opportunity for us to demonstrate our resolve in reaffirming our collective determination that noncompliance with the Treaty's core nonproliferation norms is a clear threat to international peace and security. . . .

FAST FACT

Through the Nuclear Non-Proliferation Treaty, Belarus, Kazakhstan, Libya, South Africa, and Ukraine have abandoned their nuclear weapons programs.

By secretly pursuing reprocessing and enrichment capabilities in order to produce nuclear weapons, North Korea violated both its safeguards obligations and its nonproliferation obligations under the NPT before announcing its intention to withdraw from the Treaty in 2003. In recent months, it has claimed to possess nuclear weapons.

For almost two decades Iran has conducted a clandestine nuclear weapons program, aided by the illicit network of [rogue scientist] A. Q. Khan. After two and a half years of investigation by the IAEA and adoption of no fewer than seven decisions by the IAEA Board of Governors calling on Iran to cooperate fully with the IAEA in resolving outstanding issues with its nuclear program, many questions remain unanswered. Even today, Iran persists in not cooperating fully. Iran has made clear its determination to retain the nuclear infrastructure it secretly built in violation of its NPT safeguards obligations, and is continuing to develop its nuclear capabilities around the margins of the suspension it agreed to last November [2004], for example, by continuing construction of the heavy water reactor at Arak, along with supporting infrastructure. . . .

Bolstering the NPT

[In 2004], President Bush proposed an action plan to prevent further nuclear proliferation and to address each of these needs. This plan included seven specific initiatives, including the need to criminalize proliferation-related activities. In response, the UN Security Council adopted Resolution 1540, which requires states to: criminalize proliferation of weapons of mass destruction and their means of delivery by non-state actors; enact and enforce effective export controls; and secure proliferation-sensitive equipment. This is an essential step in reducing the dangers of illicit proliferation networks and of terrorist efforts to acquire weapons of mass destruction.

The United States continues to work with others to advance other elements of the President's action plan, including: . . .

- Restricting the export of sensitive technologies, particularly the spread of enrichment and reprocessing technology, which will close a key loophole in the NPT;
- Creating a special safeguards committee of the IAEA Board of Governors, which will focus the attention of the Board on issues central to the purpose of the Treaty;
- Strengthening the Proliferation Security Initiative to intercept and prevent illicit shipments of weapons of mass destruction, their delivery systems, and related materials, which is a critical adjunct to the work of the Treaty undertaken by nations acting to defeat proliferation threats; and

Nuclear Weapons Around the World

Five "nuclear weapons states" from the Nuclear Non-Proliferation Treaty

Other known nuclear powers

States formerly possessing nuclear weapons

States suspected of being in the process of developing nuclear weapons and/or nuclear programs

States which at one point had nuclear weapons and/or nuclear weapons research programs

States claiming to possess nuclear weapons

Source: http://en.wikipedia.org/wiki/Image:Nuclear_weapon_programs_worldwide_oct2006.png.

- Expanding the "Global Partnership" to eliminate and secure sensitive materials, including weapons of mass destruction, which broadens U.S. and Russian efforts aimed at cooperative threat reduction.

Although most of these activities call for action outside the formal framework of the NPT, they are grounded on the norms and principles of nuclear nonproliferation laid down by the Treaty. If adopted, they will each answer directly real threats to the vitality of the Treaty. . . .

The Road to a Nuclear-Free World

. . . We have eliminated thousands of nuclear weapons, eliminated an entire class of intermediate-range ballistic missiles, taken B-1 bombers out of nuclear service, reduced the number of ballistic missile submarines, drastically reduced our nuclear weapons-related domestic infrastructure, and are now eliminating our most modern and sophisticated land-based ballistic missile. We have also spent billions of dollars . . . to help other countries control and eliminate their nuclear materials. We are proud to have played a leading role in reducing nuclear arsenals. . . .

. . . The NPT is a critical tool in the global struggle against proliferation. The United States remains committed to universal adherence to the NPT, and we hope that countries still outside will join the Treaty, which they can do only as non-nuclear weapon states. However, we must remain mindful that the Treaty will not continue to advance our security in the future if we do not successfully confront the current proliferation challenges. Our common obligation is clear. This Conference offers us the opportunity to expand our understanding of these critical challenges and to seek common ground on ways to respond. In the interest of world peace and security, let us work together to preserve and strengthen the NPT.

EVALUATING THE AUTHOR'S ARGUMENTS:

Stephen G. Rademaker is the assistant secretary of state for arms control—a government employee. Does knowing his background influence your opinion of his argument? If so, in what way? Clarify your answer.

The Nuclear Non-Proliferation Treaty Cannot Prevent the Spread of Weapons of Mass Destruction

Liaquat Ali Khan

"Despite its grandiose universality . . . the [Nuclear Non-Proliferation Treaty] is poised to fall apart in the near future."

In the following viewpoint Liaquat Ali Khan argues that the Nuclear Non-Proliferation Treaty (NPT) has not stopped nations from possessing nuclear weapons. In fact, Khan writes, just five nations possessed WMDs when the treaty was created thirty-five years ago. Now, however, there are nine nations with nuclear weapons, and more are furtively working to join the nuclear club. Khan also accuses the treaty of having unclear provisions regarding whether countries can pursue nuclear energy for peaceful means. Finally, Khan claims that the logic of the treaty encourages nations to seek out nuclear technology in order to protect themselves against attack from the nuclear powers. For

Liaquat Ali Khan, "Nuclear Non-Proliferation Treaty Poised to Fall Apart," *Counterpunch*, May 4, 2005. Reproduced by permission.

these reasons, Khan concludes, the NPT is no longer a useful tool for preventing the spread of nuclear weapons.

Ali Khan is a professor of law at Washburn University School of Law in Topeka, Kansas. He is the author of *A Theory of International Terrorism.*

AS YOU READ, CONSIDER THE FOLLOWING QUESTIONS:
1. What five nations are authorized by the NPT to own nuclear weapons, according to the author?
2. Why does Khan describe the NPT as a "double-headed monster?"
3. According to Khan, what did the Iraq War demonstrate about nations without nuclear weapons?

Recognizing "the devastation that would be visited upon all mankind" by a nuclear war, the Treaty on the Non-Proliferation of Nuclear Weapons (NPT) was designed to prevent the spread of nuclear weapons. The NPT, which is now 35 years old, has succeeded to the extent that nearly 190 states have subscribed to it. Despite its grandiose universality, however, here are five reasons why the NPT is poised to fall apart in the near future.

The NPT Is Easily Broken
The NPT's nuclear club has been broken into. In 1970, the Treaty divided the world into two camps: haves and have-nots. It acknowledged that five states—US, UK, France, Russia & China—lawfully possessed nuclear weapons. It

FAST FACT

Despite requiring nations not to produce nuclear weapons, Iran, Iraq, and Libya all signed the Nuclear Non-Proliferation Treaty and then cheated by continuing their WMD programs (Libya has since responded to diplomatic pressure and abandoned its program). North Korea signed and then withdrew from the treaty in 2003 and became a nuclear power in 2006.

During his presidential campaign, John Kerry expressed concerns about the rise of nuclear threats from Iran and North Korea.

hoped that the rest of the world would not acquire them. That did not happen. In 1998, India and Pakistan detonated nuclear weapons in [the] face of the world. The US now publicly admits that Israel possesses nuclear weapons. Probability dictates that North Korea has them too. The dilemma is therefore insurmountable. If the club of five is expanded to eight and perhaps more, proliferation would seem to have been accommodated. If not, the club would be treated as a foolish anomaly. Either way, the NPT is in legal disarray.

The NPT can be lawfully dumped. It allows a signatory state to withdraw from the non-proliferation regime "if it decides that extraordinary events, related to the subject matter of this Treaty, have jeopardized the supreme interests of its country." All that is required is a three months advance notice. North Korea joined the NPT in 1985. In January, 2003, however, it withdrew from the Treaty (effective immediately). If North Korea detonates the bomb and joins the de facto club, the NPT would be further weakened. And the dumping

Worldwide Nuclear Testing, 1945–2006

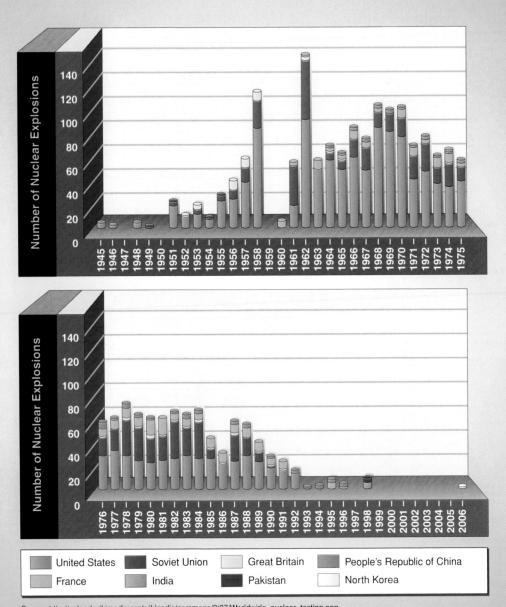

Source: http://upload.wikimedia.org/wikipedia/commons/2/27/Worldwide_nuclear_testing.png.

rule will be reaffirmed in international law. As luck would have it, there will be new withdrawals from the NPT, most likely in the Middle East where states will not accept Israel's regional nuclear monopoly. Even one or two more withdrawals will kill the Treaty.

Broken Promises and Unequal Rights

The NPT's foundational promise is not kept. The five declared nuclear-weapon states promised to cease the nuclear arms race and head toward a complete nuclear disarmament under strict and effective international control. The collapse of the Soviet Union was a godsend that [stopped] the superpowers' nuclear arms race. But no good faith effort,

as the Treaty requires, is being made towards complete nuclear disarmament. In fact, contrary to the letter and spirit of the NPT, the Bush administration is actively considering [the development of] brand new nuclear bunker-buster weapons. No treaty regime can succeed on such blatant contempt for the world. When the shepherd on the white horse loses his way, no sheep come home.

The NPT is a double-headed monster. It is simultaneously good and evil. The Treaty allows the development of nuclear energy for peaceful purposes. In fact, the Treaty rests on a bargain. States relinquished the right to have nuclear weapons because they were led to believe that "peaceful applications" of nuclear explosions will be made available to them. Iran, [which] signed the NPT, claims that it has "the unalienable right" to develop peaceful nuclear energy. The United States claims that if Iran is allowed to acquire nuclear technology, it would come closer to developing nuclear weapons. Both claims are simultaneously accurate. This double-headedness is precisely the inherent flaw of the NPT. Its one head spews light, the other flames.

A Foolish Treaty in a Dangerous World

The NPT is a suicide pact. The US foreign policy has created a global context in which it is far more protective for states to have nuclear weapons than not to have them. The war on Iraq demonstrates that a state without weapons of mass destruction is vulnerable to invasion and occupation. It would be perfectly logical to conclude that Iraq was attacked not because it had weapons of mass destruction but because it had none. This pathological logic will be further confirmed if the United States continues to pursue diplomacy with North Korea that presumably has both nuclear weapons and missiles to deliver them. The Iraq/North Korea binary reality resurrects old truths that might is right, and be firm with the bullies. And so, in a dangerous world, adhering to the NPT will be considered foolish.

For these five reasons, the NPT seems no longer viable. If the analysis above is dark and pessimistic, and something can indeed be done about the weapons of mass destruction, beware, more wars and "the devastation that would be visited upon all mankind" might be on the way. A complete nuclear disarmament is, of course, another possible solution.

EVALUATING THE AUTHORS' ARGUMENTS:

In this viewpoint Liaquat Ali Khan argues that the war in Iraq showed nations such as Iran and North Korea that they need to own nuclear weapons in order to avoid being attacked by the United States. Considering what you know on the topic, what is your opinion of this argument? Do you think that the war in Iraq helped deter nations from producing weapons of mass destruction or actually encouraged more nations to develop WMDs in self-defense? Use evidence found in this book to back up your answer.

International Cooperation Will Prevent the Spread of Weapons of Mass Destruction

"Every civilized nation has a stake in preventing the spread of weapons of mass destruction."

George W. Bush

In the following viewpoint George W. Bush argues that it is the responsibility of the entire civilized world to prevent the spread of weapons of mass destruction (WMDs). He calls on nations to uphold international laws that prohibit the development and trafficking of nuclear weapons technology. He also encourages nations to respect and support the Nuclear Non-Proliferation Treaty, an international treaty that seeks to curb the spread of WMDs. Bush concludes that WMDs pose a threat to everyone on earth, and thus all nations on earth must work together to eradicate the danger.

George W. Bush is the forty-third president of the United States.

George W. Bush, "Remarks by the President on Weapons of Mass Destruction Proliferation," White House, February 11, 2004.

AS YOU READ, CONSIDER THE FOLLOWING QUESTIONS:

1. What changes would Bush like to see made to the Proliferation Security Initiative (PSI)?
2. What does Bush suggest the forty nations of the Nuclear Suppliers Group should refuse to do?
3. Why does Bush believe Iran should not be allowed to serve on the IAEA Board of Governors?

On September the 11th, 2001, America and the world witnessed a new kind of war. We saw the great harm that a stateless network could inflict upon our country; killers armed with box cutters, mace, and 19 airline tickets. Those attacks also raised the prospect of even worse dangers—of other weapons in the hands of other men. The greatest threat before humanity today is the possibility of secret and sudden attack with chemical or biological or radiological or nuclear weapons. . . .

America, and the entire civilized world, will face this threat for decades to come. We must confront the danger with open eyes, and unbending purpose. I have made clear to all the policy of this nation: America will not permit terrorists and dangerous regimes to threaten us with the world's most deadly weapons. . . .

Acting Together to Be Effective

There is a consensus among nations that proliferation cannot be tolerated. Yet this consensus means little unless it is translated into action. Every civilized nation has a stake in preventing the spread of weapons of mass destruction. These materials and technologies, and the people who traffic in them, cross many borders. To stop this trade, the nations of the world must be strong and determined. We must work together, we must act effectively. Today, I announce seven proposals to strengthen the world's efforts to stop the spread of deadly weapons.

First, I propose that the work of the Proliferation Security Initiative be expanded to address more than shipments and transfers [of nuclear material]. Building on the tools we've developed to fight terrorists, we can take direct action against proliferation networks. We need greater cooperation not just among intelligence and military services, but in law enforcement, as well. PSI participants and other willing nations should use the Interpol and all other means to bring to justice those who traffic in deadly weapons, to shut down their labs, to seize their materials, to freeze their assets. We must act on every lead. We will find the middlemen, the suppliers and the buyers. Our message to proliferators must be consistent and it must be clear: We will find you, and we're not going to rest until you are stopped.

Second, I call on all nations to strengthen the laws and international controls that govern proliferation. At the U.N. [in 2003], I proposed a new Security Council resolution requiring all states to criminalize proliferation, enact strict export controls, and secure all sensitive materials within their borders. The Security Council should pass this proposal quickly. And when they do, America stands ready to help

Chief UN weapons inspector Richard Butler, left, shakes hands with Iraqi foreign minister Tariq Aziz. President Bush believes that nations, working together, can prevent the spread of nuclear weapons by strengthening and enforcing international laws on proliferation.

other governments to draft and enforce the new laws that will help us deal with proliferation.

Preventing the International Spread of WMDs

Third, I propose to expand our efforts to keep weapons from the Cold War and other dangerous materials out of the wrong hands. In 1991, Congress passed the Nunn-Lugar legislation. Senator Lugar had a clear vision, along with Senator Nunn, about what to do with the old Soviet Union. Under this program, we're helping former Soviet states find productive employment for former weapons scientists. We're dismantling, destroying and securing weapons and materials left over from the Soviet WMD arsenal. We have more work to do there.

FAST FACT

Only one nation has ever used nuclear weapons in wartime: the United States, when it dropped atomic bombs on Japan in World War II.

And as a result of the G-8 Summit in 2002, we agreed to provide $20 billion over 10 years—half of it from the United States—to support such programs. We should expand this cooperation elsewhere in the world. We will retain WMD scientists and technicians in countries like Iraq and Libya. We will help nations end the use of weapons-grade uranium in research reactors. I urge more nations to contribute to these efforts. The nations of the world must do all we can to secure and eliminate nuclear and chemical and biological and radiological materials.

We Must Close Nuclear Loopholes

As we track and destroy these networks, we must also prevent governments from developing nuclear weapons under false pretenses. The Nuclear Non-Proliferation Treaty was designed more than 30 years ago to prevent the spread of nuclear weapons beyond those states which already possessed them. Under this treaty, nuclear states agreed to help non-nuclear states develop peaceful atomic energy if they renounced the pursuit of nuclear weapons. But the treaty has a loophole which has been exploited by nations such as North Korea and Iran. These regimes are allowed to produce nuclear material that can be used to build bombs under the cover of civilian nuclear programs.

So today, as a fourth step, I propose a way to close the loophole. The world must create a safe, orderly system to field civilian nuclear plants without adding to the danger of weapons proliferation. The world's leading nuclear exporters should ensure that states have reliable access at reasonable cost to fuel for civilian reactors, so long as those states renounce enrichment and reprocessing. Enrichment and reprocessing are not necessary for nations seeking to harness nuclear energy for peaceful purposes.

Rules All Nations Must Follow

The 40 nations of the Nuclear Suppliers Group should refuse to sell enrichment and reprocessing equipment and technologies to any state that does not already possess full-scale, functioning enrichment and reprocessing plants. This step will prevent new states from developing the means to produce fissile material for nuclear bombs. Proliferators must not be allowed to cynically manipulate the NPT to acquire the material and infrastructure necessary for manufacturing illegal weapons.

For international norms to be effective, they must be enforced. It is the charge of the International Atomic Energy Agency to uncover banned nuclear activity around the world and report those violations to the U.N. Security Council. We must ensure that the IAEA has all the tools it needs to fulfill its essential mandate. America and other nations support what is called the Additional Protocol, which requires states to declare a broad range of nuclear activities and facilities, and allow the IAEA to inspect those facilities. . . .

And, finally, countries under investigation for violating nuclear non-proliferation obligations are currently allowed to serve on the IAEA Board of Governors. For instance, Iran—a country suspected of maintaining an extensive nuclear weapons program—recently completed a two-year term on the Board. Allowing potential violators to serve on the Board creates an unacceptable barrier to effective action. No state under investigation for proliferation violations should be allowed to serve on the IAEA Board of Governors—or on the new

Nuclear Explosion Milestones

The following list is of milestone nuclear explosions. The first nuclear test of a given weapon type for a country is included, as well as tests which were notable (such as the largest test ever) and TNT yield.

Date	Name	Yield (kilotons)	Country	Significance
Jul. 16, 1945	*Trinity*	19	USA	First fission weapon test
Aug. 6, 1945	*Little Boy*	15	USA	Bombing of Hiroshima, Japan
Aug. 9, 1945	*Fat Man*	21	USA	Bombing of Nagasaki, Japan
Aug. 29, 1949	*Joe 1*	22	USSR	First fission weapon test by the USSR
Oct. 3, 1952	*Hurricane*	25	UK	First fission weapon test by the UK
Nov. 1, 1952	*Ivy Mike*	10,200	USA	First staged thermonuclear weapon test (not deployable)
Aug. 12, 1953	*Joe 4*	400	USSR	First fusion weapon test by the USSR (not staged but deployable)
Mar. 1, 1954	*Castle Bravo*	15,000	USA	First deployable staged thermonuclear weapon; fallout accident
Nov. 22, 1955	*RDS-37*	1,600	USSR	First staged thermonuclear weapon test by the USSR (deployable)
Nov. 8, 1957	*Grapple X*	1,800	UK	First (successful) staged thermonuclear weapon test by the UK
Feb. 13, 1960	*Gerboise Bleue*	60	France	First fission weapon test by France
Oct. 31, 1961	*Tsar Bomba*	50,000	USSR	Largest thermonuclear weapon ever tested
Oct. 16, 1964	*596*	22	China	First fission weapon test by China
Jun. 17, 1967	*Test No. 6*	3,300	China	First staged thermonuclear weapon test by China
Aug. 24, 1968	*Canopus*	2,600	France	First staged thermonuclear test by France
May 18, 1974	*Smiling Buddha*	12	India	First fission nuclear explosive test by India
May 11, 1998	*Shakti I*	43	India	First potential fusion/boosted weapon test by India (exact yield disputed, between 25kt and 45kt)
May 13, 1998	*Shakti II*	12	India	First fission weapon test by India
May 28, 1998	*Chagai-I*	9	Pakistan	First fission weapon test by Pakistan
Oct. 9, 2006	*Hwadae-ri*	Less than 1	North Korea	First fission device tested by North Korea

special committee. And any state currently on the Board that comes under investigation should be suspended from the Board. The integrity and mission of the IAEA depends on this simple principle: Those actively breaking the rules should not be entrusted with enforcing the rules.

A Task for the World

As we move forward to address these challenges we will consult with our friends and allies on all these new measures. We will listen to their ideas. Together we will defend the safety of all nations and preserve the peace of the world.

Over the last two years, a great coalition has come together to defeat terrorism and to oppose the spread of weapons of mass destruction—the inseparable commitments of the war on terror. We've shown that proliferators can be discovered and can be stopped. We've shown that for regimes that choose defiance, there are serious consequences. The way ahead is not easy, but it is clear. We will proceed as if the lives of our citizens depend on our vigilance, because they do. Terrorists and terror states are in a race for weapons of mass murder, a race they must lose. Terrorists are resourceful; we're more resourceful. They're determined; we must be more determined. We will never lose focus or resolve. We'll be unrelenting in the defense of free nations, and rise to the hard demands of dangerous times.

EVALUATING THE AUTHORS' ARGUMENTS:

In this viewpoint George W. Bush argues that it is the responsibility of the entire world to confront the threat posed by WMDs. In particular he warns against letting WMDs fall into the hands of terrorists and rogue nations. Bush calls this problem the "greatest threat before humanity today." Considering what you know on the subject, do you agree with Bush's assessment of the problem? Are weapons of mass destruction humanity's greatest threat, or is it an exaggerated and manageable problem? Explain your answer using evidence from other viewpoints in this book.

Nothing Can Prevent the Spread of Weapons of Mass Destruction

William Langewiesche

"It is important to recognize that the spread of nuclear weapons is a condition over which we do not have control and for which there is no solution."

In the following viewpoint author William Langewiesche argues that nothing can prevent the spread of weapons of mass destruction (WMDs), and the best thing the United States can do is to adjust to the realities of living in a nuclear world. The United States and other nuclear powers developed WMDs for protection, Langewiesche reminds readers. It is therefore hypocritical, he says, for them to tell poorer, weaker nations that they are not allowed to possess such technology for protection too. The United States should focus its energy not on preventing states from becoming nuclear powers but from selling their nuclear technology to terrorists, Langewiesche concludes.

William Langewiesche is a reporter whose articles have appeared in the *Atlantic Monthly* and the *Los Angeles Times*, from which this viewpoint is taken. He is also the author of *American Ground: Unbuilding the World Trade Center* and *The Outlaw Sea: A World of Freedom, Chaos, and Crime*.

AS YOU READ, CONSIDER THE FOLLOWING QUESTIONS:
1. Name four founding members of the Federation of American (Atomic) Scientists (FAS) and describe their message to the world about weapons of mass destruction.
2. According to the author, what effect do international sanctions or incentives have on deterring the desire for WMDs?
3. What does the author think is the surest recipe for self-destruction and disaster?

There is no doubt that the acquisition of atomic weapons by North Korea is the worst development yet in the ongoing story of nuclear proliferation by upstart states. The regime in Pyongyang is arguably the spookiest in the world today—bellicose, repressive, unstable and so mentally isolated that it sometimes appears to be outright insane. A nuclear North Korea is definitely a dangerous place; it increases the chances in Asia for all sorts of trouble and threatens to kick off a regional arms race. This needs to be acknowledged.

Nonetheless, what's done is done, and though we may protest and bluster, there is very little the U.S. can do to stop it from proceeding. Rather than making a show of our weakness, we would do well to calm down. After all, this was not unexpected; the fact is, the spread of nuclear weapons is, and always has been, inevitable.

The Nuclear Age Is upon Us

A little perspective might help. In the months after World War II, a group of men responsible for producing the atomic bomb—including Albert Einstein, J. Robert Oppenheimer, Niels Bohr, Leo Szilard and others—created the Federation of American (Atomic) Scientists, or FAS, to educate the public about this new breed of weapon. Washington at the time harbored the illusion that it possessed a great secret and could keep the bomb for itself.

The founders of the FAS disagreed. They argued that with the destruction of Hiroshima and Nagasaki, any engineering doubts had been emphatically answered and, because the basic science of nuclear reactions was already widely known, other nations could invest in nuclear programs and be certain of the returns. There were any number of physicists and engineers worldwide capable of guiding them through the process. FAS members warned the American people in stark and simple terms. In essence, they said that the whole world would soon be nuclear-armed. There is no secret here, they said, and there is also no defense. The Nuclear Age is upon us, and it cannot be undone.

They got the timing wrong. Nuclear proliferation did proceed, but for 50 years it was slowed (and in some cases stopped) by diplomacy and, more fundamentally, by the Cold War itself, with the guarantees it offered to nonnuclear nations of surrogate nuclear strength under the U.S. and Soviet retaliatory "umbrellas."

The Desire for Nuclear Weapons

Since then, however, the umbrellas have frayed, and the world has become a more fractured and complicated place, no longer bound by the old alliances, where independent nuclear arsenals have greater meaning than before. Paradoxically, the desire for nuclear weapons is spreading in inverse relation to the lowered risk of an all-out global nuclear war. This is a trend that began even before the fall of the Soviet Union, but it is accelerating in a world where countries must turn to themselves for protection and where the U.S., especially after the invasion of Iraq, is seen as an aggressor and a threat. For these reasons and others, new nuclear players are emerging to challenge the rules of the game.

What the new players have in common is that they are poor and undeveloped nations, with weak economies and precarious political systems. If this seems counterintuitive, consider the fact that nuclear weapons are not only simple but cheap.

Earlier this year [in 2006] in Moscow, a Russian nuclear official put it this way to me: "Nuclear weapons technology has become a useful tool, especially for the weak. It allows them to satisfy their ambitions without much expense. If they want to intimidate others, to be respect-

Some believe it is hypocritical for the existing nuclear powers to prevent other nations from attaining nuclear weapons.

ed by others, this is now the easiest way to do it." Once a country decides to become a nuclear weapons power, he said, it will do so regardless of international sanctions or incentives.

Oppenheimer warned of this implicitly 60 years earlier. He wrote in 1945: "Atomic explosives vastly increase the power of destruction per dollar spent, per man-hour invested; they profoundly upset the precarious balance between the effort necessary to destroy, and the extent of the destruction. . . . None of the uncertainties can becloud the fact it will cost enormously less to destroy a square mile with atomic weapons than with any weapons hitherto known to warfare."

Oppenheimer talked about it in terms of the "evil that a dollar can do," but of course, one person's definition of evil may be another's definition of self-defense—or, more generally, a demand for equality among nations. The most succinct criticism of the Nuclear Nonproliferation Treaty came from the Argentines when they refused to sign it, that it amounted to "the disarmament of the disarmed."

Everyone Has the Right to Self-Defense

In Islamabad [Pakistan], an official close to the nuclear-armed Musharraf regime said to me: "The best way to fight proliferation is to pursue global disarmament. Fine, great, sure—if you expect that to happen. But you cannot have a world order in which you have five or eight nuclear weapons states on the one hand, and the rest of the international community on the other. There are many places like Pakistan, poor countries which have legitimate security concerns—every bit as legitimate as yours. And yet you ask them to address those concerns without nuclear weapons, while you have nuclear weapons, and you have everything else? It is not a question of what is fair, or right or wrong. It is simply not going to work."

The man was right. When focused on the U.S., his point becomes an argument not for standing down from the diplomacy of nonproliferation but for finding the courage to accept the dangers of a changing world in which new countries have acquired nuclear weapons, and some may actually use them.

Has North Korea joined the ranks of nuclear powers? If so, so be it. There will be other nuclear newcomers in the decades to come. Iran will be next, but it will not be the last. Turkey, Syria and Saudi Arabia are believed to be interested and could easily proceed, depending on regional events. So could Algeria. So could Brazil and Venezuela. The future is unknowable, but there is no limit to where these weapons could spread.

Learning to Live in a Nuclear World

The good news, however perversely, is that no nuclear-armed regime (and certainly not Iran's) is likely to be as reckless as North Korea's. In that sense, the developments in North Korea can serve as an exercise not in stopping nuclear proliferation but in learning how to live with it after it occurs. The ideal, of course, would be to desist from policies of preemptive invasion and to engage the upstart powers respectfully through economic and diplomatic ties.

If that is not feasible, however, other options exist, based on the premise that nuclear weapons are defensive in nature and that regimes even as strange as Pyongyang's are generally fairly conventional players with infrastructures at risk and subject to restraint through the guarantee of retaliatory strikes.

No Nuclear Access for Terrorists

There is one move we can make right now that would sharply reduce, if not eliminate, another risk: that a regime like North Korea's or Iran's might hand off a functional bomb to stateless terrorists who, with nothing to lose, would have every reason to use it. We can make it emphatically clear that if we or our most important friends are ever hit by terrorists with a ready-made nuclear device, we will immediately devastate whatever regime is to blame.

Ultimately, however, it is important to recognize that the spread of nuclear weapons is a condition over which we do not have control and for which there is no solution. It does no good to bemoan the folly of it all or to belabor the fact that we are the ones who ushered in the Nuclear Age. The world is an unsafe place, and we have no choice but to live in it. Pretending otherwise, or imagining that we can impose order when we lack the power to do so, is the surest recipe for self-destruction and disaster.

EVALUATING THE AUTHORS' ARGUMENTS:

In this viewpoint the author argues that nothing can prevent the spread of weapons of mass destruction, and the best thing the United States can do is to adjust to the realities of living in a nuclear world. How do you think each of the other authors in this chapter might respond to this suggestion? List each speaker and write two to three sentences on what you think their response might be.

Chapter 3

How Should Rogue Nations Who Seek Weapons of Mass Destruction Be Dealt With?

Some are concerned that an Al Qaeda presence in Pakistan could lead it to become a rogue nation.

Military Action Could Prevent Iran from Acquiring Weapons of Mass Destruction

William Kristol

"The only way diplomatic, political, and economic pressure has a chance to work over the next months is if the military option— or various military options—are kept on the table."

In the following viewpoint author William Kristol argues that world leaders must be willing to use military force to prevent Iran from developing weapons of mass destruction (WMDs). In order for diplomatic, political, and economic measures to effectively deter Iran from developing WMDs, Iran must be scared it could face military consequences if it does not comply. Too many actors are willing to accept a nuclear Iran, says Kristol, perhaps not realizing how dangerous the Iranian regime would be if it had nuclear weapons. Kristol warns that the growing threat from Iran must be countered by any means necessary—which must include the option of going to war.

William Kristol is the founder and editor of the *Weekly Standard*, a conservative newsmagazine from which this viewpoint was taken.

An unrepentant rogue state with a history of sponsoring terrorists seeks to develop weapons of mass destruction. The United States tries to work with European allies to deal with the problem peacefully, depending on International Atomic Energy Agency inspections and United Nations sanctions. The Europeans are generally hesitant and wishful. Russia and China are difficult and obstructive. Eventually the reality of the threat, the obduracy of the rogue state regime in power, becomes too obvious to be ignored.

This is not a history lesson about Iraq. These are today's headlines about Iran, where the regime is openly pursuing its ambition to become a nuclear power. "But this time diplomacy has to be given a chance to work," the doves coo. "Maybe this time Israel will take care of the problem,"[1] some hawks whisper. Both are being escapist.

Options for War Must Be Kept Open

Doves profess concern about Iran's nuclear program and endorse various diplomatic responses to it. But they don't want even to contemplate the threat of military action. Perhaps military action won't ultimately be necessary. But the only way diplomatic, political, and economic pressure has a chance to work over the next months is if the military option—or various military options—are kept on the table.

Meanwhile, some hawks, defenders of the Iraq war, would prefer to deal with one challenge at a time. They hope we can kick the can down the road a while longer, or that a *deus ex [machina]*—a Jewish one!—will appear to do our job for us. But great powers don't get to avoid their urgent responsibilities because they'd prefer to deal with

---

1. The author is referring to 1981, when Israel blew up an Iraqi nuclear weapons facility, greatly hampering Iraq's nuclear potential.

only one problem at a time, or to slough those responsibilities off onto others. To be clear: We support diplomatic, political, and economic efforts to halt the nuclear program of the Iranian regime. We support multilateral efforts through the International Atomic Energy Agency and the United Nations, and the assembling of coalitions of the willing, if necessary, to support sanctions and other forms of pressure. We support serious efforts to help democrats and dissidents in Iran, in the hope that regime change can be achieved without military action from the outside. We support strengthening our covert and intelligence capabilities. And we support holding open the possibility of, and beginning to prepare for, various forms of military action.

Too Many Are Willing to Accept a Nuclear Iran

Many people—the *New York Times* editorial board, much of Europe, even some in the Bush administration—don't really believe a nuclear Iran is unacceptable. They're of course all for various multilateral efforts to persuade [Iranian] President Ahmadinejad and Hashemi Rafsanjani,

Iraqi missiles found during the war in Iraq are transported for testing. Some are concerned that the similiarity between Iran and Iraq in their approach to weapons of mass destruction will ultimately require military action to halt the spread of Iran's nuclear program.

head of Iran's Council of Expediency, as well as Ayatollah Ali Khamenei [Iran's spiritual leader], to change their minds and abandon their nuclear ambitions. But the *Times*, and much of Europe, and some in the administration, don't really pretend that these attempts at persuasion are likely to work. At the end of the day, they think we can live with a nuclear Iran. After all, containment and deterrence worked with the Soviet Union; they could also work with Iran, one mid-level State Department official said in an unguarded moment in my presence a couple of months ago.

FAST FACT

According to a June 2006 CBS News poll, 22 percent of Americans believe military action is the best way to deal with the threat from Iran and believe that action must be taken soon.

We don't agree—and we don't think President Bush does, either. A Cuban missile crisis [in 1962] with Khrushchev's Soviet Union was bad enough. Are we willing to risk it with Ahmadinejad's Iran? What about nuclear proliferation throughout the region? What about the hopes for a liberal, less-extremist-and-terror-friendly Middle East?

Military Action Could Deter Iran

Advocates of containment and deterrence should step forward to make their case openly and honestly. We look forward to engaging them in a real debate. Right now, if you read the *Times* editorial page, or Timothy Garton Ash in the London *Guardian*, there's lots of talk about the unfortunate behavior of Iran, lots of urging of good-faith multilateral efforts—and lots of finger-wagging warnings against even thinking of military action. This isn't serious.

Others, fortunately, are more serious. The *Washington Post* editorial page, for one, endorses political and economic steps of real consequence, warns against letting diplomacy degenerate into appeasement, proposes to test the seriousness of our allies and nations like Russia and China—and refuses to rule out the threat of military action.

And President Bush and [Secretary of State] Condoleezza Rice are serious. They are now speaking with new urgency, since the Iranian

Iran's Nuclear Weapons Program

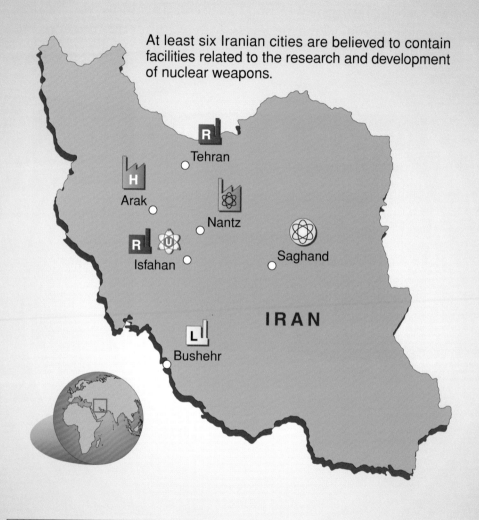

At least six Iranian cities are believed to contain facilities related to the research and development of nuclear weapons.

Tehran

Arak

Nantz

Saghand

Isfahan

IRAN

Bushehr

 Research reactors/facilities	Uranium mines	Uranium processing facility
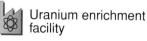 Uranium enrichment facility	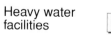 Heavy water facilities	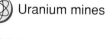 Light-water reactor

Source: www.cns.miis.edu/research/iran/images/mapbig.gif.

How Should Rogue Nations Who Seek Weapons of Mass Destruction Be Dealt With? 73

government is testing us, and its nuclear program could well be getting close to the point of no return. And they know that they have to speak with confidence and authority. Our adversaries cannot be allowed to believe that, because some of the intelligence on Iraq was bad, or because the insurgency in Iraq has been difficult, we will be at all intimidated from taking the necessary steps against the current regime in Tehran.

EVALUATING THE AUTHOR'S ARGUMENTS:

In the viewpoint you just read, William Kristol uses history, facts, and examples to make his argument that the United States should reserve the right to attack Iran if necessary. He does not, however, use any quotations to support his point. If you were to rewrite this article and insert quotations, what authorities might you quote from? Where would you place these quotations to bolster the points Kristol makes?

Military Action Should Not Be Undertaken Against Iran

M.M. Eskandari-Qajar

"Diplomacy, not war, should be the path to resolving the present dilemma [with Iran]."

In 2005 Iran restarted its nuclear weapons program against the wishes of the international community. In the following viewpoint, M.M. Eskandari-Qajar argues the United States should not militarily attack Iran for its actions. Eskandari-Qajar explains why Iran wants weapons of mass destruction—it feels that acquiring such weapons is the only way to deter an American attack against it. The author believes that Iran is only acting in self-defense and is not likely to start any wars. Furthermore, an attack against Iran would be more difficult than the attack against Iraq; the author argues that the United States is incapable of occupying Iran and establishing postwar peace there. For these reasons Eskandari-Qajar concludes that the conflict with Iran should be resolved diplomatically, not militarily.

M.M. Eskandari-Qajar is associate professor of political science and Middle Eastern history and chair of the political science department at Santa Barbara City College, California.

AS YOU READ, CONSIDER THE FOLLOWING QUESTIONS:
1. According to the author, how close is Iran to being able to build nuclear weapons?
2. Name three acts of aggression the United States has taken against Iran, as described by Eskandari-Qajar.
3. In what condition is the Iranian military, according to the author?

G iven the current tensions between Iran and the United States over Iran's resumption of its nuclear program, we would do well to reflect on the following truths and allow ourselves to gain perspective and distance from the frenzy of news reports about imminent war with or by Iran.

The first principle of international relations is that countries seek to protect their interests by whatever means they can. The second principle is that countries do so as rational actors intent on bringing about gain, or if not gain, at least avoidance of loss. These are observable facts of international politics. How countries go about achieving these aims differs from country to country, but the fact remains that countries act this way in their relations with each other. Moreover, most of the interactions between countries in the world are peaceful or, to be more precise, are actions short of war. War and warlike actions are the exception and are rarely engaged in, though it certainly seems otherwise, since war looms so large in our collective psyche.

The Threat from Iran

This said, let us look at what events led to the present tensions. On October 26, 2005, at the Islamic Summit in Saudi Arabia, during a conference titled World without Zionism, the President of Iran, Mahmoud Ahmadinejad, quoting the late Ayatollah Khomeini, stated that "Israel should be wiped off the face of the earth." In that same speech, he also said the Holocaust was a "myth." Then, [in January 2006], the Iranian government decided to break the seals placed on three of its nuclear facilities by UN inspectors and to resume work at those facilities despite the call by the international community to desist.

These remarks, combined with the latest moves to restart the nuclear program in Iran—a program, incidentally, the early components of which were supplied to Iran by the United States during the rule of the late Shah—have put Israel on edge and the U.S. in a position to push more urgently for a censure of Iran by the UN Security Council and an imposition of sanctions by that body. The fear, of course, is that Iran is working on a nuclear bomb and not just on nuclear energy as it claims. A nuclear Iran with stated intentions to wipe Israel off the map is an untenable situation for any country in the region, let alone Israel. A nuclear exchange in the Middle East would mean the destruction of several countries and the death of millions of people far beyond the two countries in question. The sheer thought of it boggles the mind and makes one recoil in horror, but we must remind ourselves that this is not where things stand at the moment.

Unless security services in the U.S. and Israel know differently, according to UN inspectors and nuclear technology experts, Iran is a few thousand centrifuges short of the capacity to weaponize uranium. Should Iran ever be capable of achieving this feat, the consensus is that this is years away. What is clear, though, is that Iran wishes to complete its nuclear energy program and gain the respect this technological achievement is thought to bring. Additionally, Iran wishes to have the capacity to at least hint at the possibility of military nuclear capability as a deterrent, given its precarious situation in the Middle East. The question is: Why does Iran feel this way? To understand that, let us for a moment see the situation from Iran's point of view.

> **FAST FACT**
>
> According to a May 2006 Fox News/Opinion Dynamics poll, 74 percent of respondents believe the United Nations cannot stop Iran from acquiring the technology to build weapons of mass destruction.

Understanding Iran's Desire for WMDs

Iran and the U.S. have been at odds for almost three decades now. Since the 1979 Revolution and the hostage crisis of 1980, Iran has

Some claim that Iran's desire for nuclear weapons is a reaction to a threat of attack from the United States.

been on the pariah list of the United States. As a result of its dislike of the Iranian regime, the U.S. even supported [Iraqi dictator] Saddam Hussein in his brutal eight-year war against Iran in the 1980s. In 2002, in his State of the Union Address, President [George W.] Bush famously put Iran on the "Axis of Evil," along with Iraq and North Korea, and then proceeded to deal with Iraq militarily. Prior to this, in response to the September 11 attacks, the U.S. retaliated against Afghanistan, shattering the Taliban regime and putting [terrorist Osama] bin Laden on the run. Simultaneously, the U.S. built up its Persian Gulf bases in Qatar, Bahrain, Kuwait, and Saudi Arabia, and managed to forge military alliances with Uzbekistan, Kyrgyzstan, and Tadjikistan in its war on terror. The U.S. also built an alliance with the government of Pakistan, the only Islamic government with a known nuclear arsenal. On Iran's western flank, America's strongest ally in the region, Turkey, stands ready as both a NATO member and a staunch ally of Israel as well. Finally, Azerbaijan and even Georgia, with Russia's blessing, have asked for U.S. military troop presence in their countries.

Looking at this situation from the point of view of the Iranian government, Iran finds itself surrounded on all sides by countries with large contingents of U.S. troops and finds itself on the "to-be-dealt-with" list of the United States. Given this scenario, Iran needs to find a way to stave off the handwriting on the wall. The present moves by Iran should be interpreted in this light and no more. As belligerent as the rhetoric of Iran may have been toward Israel, and as rash a move as the removal of the seals and the resumption of work at the nuclear facilities may be, the United States needs to understand that a military move against Iran either by itself or by one of its allies in the region would spell disaster for the region as a whole. Iran is not Iraq. Iraq was weakened by 10 years of military and economic embargos. Iran's armed forces, having acquired missiles and having been tested by fire in the longest war in the region, are stronger and far better equipped today than they were under the Shah.

Diplomacy, Not War

Were America to take preemptive action, America would also have to be willing and ready to occupy Iran to diffuse Iran's anger at having been struck. Even if it were possible to pacify a nation the size of Iran after such an attack, given its global commitments, America is in no position now to do that and thus cooler heads must prevail and remind the world that Iran's moves are to be expected given its situation and should not be taken for more than they are. Diplomacy, not war, should be the path to resolving the present dilemma.

Sanctions Will Force North Korea to Give Up Its Weapons of Mass Destruction

"The Security Council ... condemns the nuclear test proclaimed by the DPRK on 9 October 2006 in flagrant disregard of its relevant resolutions."

United Nations Security Council Draft Resolution 1718

The following viewpoint is text from the United Nations Security Council Draft Resolution 1718, the document that imposed sanctions on North Korea following its October 2006 nuclear weapons test. In a rare show of unity, the United Nations Security Council (composed of five permanent member states—the United States, Russia, China, the United Kingdom, and France—and ten rotating member states) voted unanimously to impose the sanctions. Under these rules, no member state is allowed to supply North Korea with military supplies or any other materials that could help it continue its weapons program. It also prevented the trade of luxury goods as a way to punish the North

United Nations Security Council, "United Nations Security Council Draft Resolution 1718 S/2006/805," United Nations Security Council, October 14, 2006. Reprinted with the permission of the United Nations.

Korean leadership for its violation of UN rules. The UN adopted the resolution to punish North Korea's defiance, to prevent it from further developing its weapons program, to pressure it to return to international talks, and to show other nations that are considering developing nuclear weapons that there are consequences for violating international laws.

AS YOU READ, CONSIDER THE FOLLOWING QUESTIONS:
1. What three specific demands does the United Nations Security Council make of North Korea?
2. What types of military supplies does UN Resolution 1718 prohibit North Korea from acquiring through trade?
3. What actions does the resolution require member states to do?

The Security Council, . . .

Reaffirming that proliferation of nuclear, chemical and biological weapons, as well as their means of delivery, constitutes a threat to international peace and security,

Expressing the gravest concern at the claim by the Democratic People's Republic of Korea (DPRK) that it has conducted a test of a nuclear weapon on 9 October 2006, and at the challenge such a test constitutes to the Treaty on the Non-Proliferation of Nuclear Weapons and to international efforts aimed at strengthening the global regime of non-proliferation of nuclear weapons, and the danger it poses to peace and stability in the region and beyond,

Expressing its firm conviction that the international regime on the non-proliferation of nuclear weapons should be maintained and recalling that the DPRK cannot have the status of a nuclear-weapon state in accordance with the Treaty on the Non-Proliferation of Nuclear Weapons,

Deploring the DPRK's announcement of withdrawal from the Treaty on the Non-Proliferation of Nuclear Weapons and its pursuit of nuclear weapons,

Deploring further that the DPRK has refused to return to the Six-Party talks without precondition, . . .

North Korea's Nuclear Facilities

In the last 50 years, North Korea has managed to exploit its own uranium mines and a growing base of nuclear physicists to create a nuclear weapons research program.

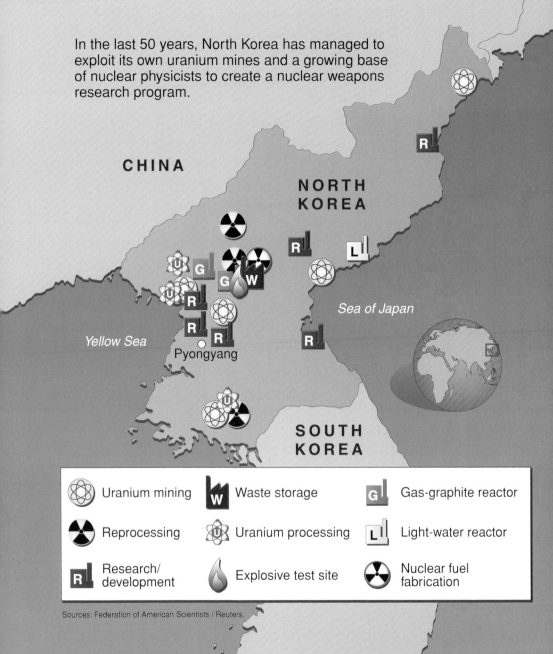

CHINA

NORTH KOREA

Sea of Japan

Yellow Sea

Pyongyang

SOUTH KOREA

⚛	Uranium mining	🏭W	Waste storage	G	Gas-graphite reactor
☢	Reprocessing	⚛U	Uranium processing	L	Light-water reactor
R	Research/ development	💧	Explosive test site	☢	Nuclear fuel fabrication

Sources: Federation of American Scientists / Reuters.

Underlining the importance that the DPRK respond to other security and humanitarian concerns of the international community,

Expressing profound concern that the test claimed by the DPRK has generated increased tension in the region and beyond, and *determining* therefore that there is a clear threat to international peace and security, . . .

North Korea's Actions Cannot Be Tolerated

1. *Condemns* the nuclear test proclaimed by the DPRK on 9 October 2006 in flagrant disregard of its relevant resolutions, . . . including that such a test would bring universal condemnation of the international community and would represent a clear threat to international peace and security;

2. *Demands* that the DPRK not conduct any further nuclear test or launch of a ballistic missile;

3. *Demands* that the DPRK immediately retract its announcement of withdrawal from the Treaty on the Non-Proliferation of Nuclear Weapons;

4. *Demands* further that the DPRK return to the Treaty on the Non-Proliferation of Nuclear Weapons and International Atomic Energy Agency (IAEA) safeguards, and *underlines* the need for all States Parties to the Treaty on the Non-Proliferation of Nuclear Weapons to continue to comply with their Treaty obligations;

5. *Decides* that the DPRK shall suspend all activities related to its ballistic missile programme and in this context re-establish its pre-existing commitments to a moratorium on missile launching;

6. *Decides* that the DPRK shall abandon all nuclear weapons and existing nuclear programmes in a complete, verifiable and irreversible manner, shall act strictly in accordance with the obligations applicable to parties under the Treaty on the Non-Proliferation of Nuclear Weapons and the terms and conditions of its International Atomic Energy Agency (IAEA) Safeguards Agreement (IAEA INFCIRC/403) and shall provide the IAEA transparency measures extending beyond these requirements, including such access to individuals, documentation, equipments

and facilities as may be required and deemed necessary by the IAEA;

7. *Decides* also that the DPRK shall abandon all other existing weapons of mass destruction and ballistic missile programmes in a complete, verifiable and irreversible manner;

Sanctions Must Be Imposed on North Korea

8. *Decides* that:

(a) all Member States shall prevent the direct or indirect supply, sale or transfer to the DPRK, through their territories or by their nationals, or using their flag vessels or aircraft, and whether or not originating in their territories, of:

1. any battle tanks, armoured combat vehicles, large calibre artillery systems, combat aircraft, attack helicopters, warships, missiles or missile systems as defined for the purpose of the United Nations Register on Conventional Arms, or related materiel including spare parts. . . .

2. all items, materials, equipment, goods and technology . . . determined by the Security Council or the Committee, which could contribute to DPRK's nuclear-related, ballistic missile-related or other weapons of mass destruction-related programmes;

3. luxury goods; . . .

Freezing Funds, Preventing Trade, and Inspecting Cargo

(d) all Member States shall, in accordance with their respective legal processes, freeze immediately the funds, other financial assets and economic resources which are on their territories at the date of the adoption of this resolution or at any time thereafter, that are owned or controlled, directly or indirectly, by the persons or entities designated by the Committee or by the Security Council as being engaged in or providing support for, including through other illicit means, DPRK's nuclear-related, other weapons of mass destruction-related and ballistic missile-related programmes, or by persons or entities acting on their behalf or at their direction, and ensure that any funds, financial assets or economic resources are prevented from being made available by their nationals or by any persons or entities within their territories, to or for the benefit of such persons or entities;

(e) all Member States shall take the necessary steps to prevent the entry into or transit through their territories of the persons designated by the Committee or by the Security Council as being responsible for, including through supporting or promoting, DPRK policies in relation to the DPRK's nuclear-related, ballistic missile-related and other weapons of mass destruction-related programmes, together with their family members, provided that nothing in this paragraph shall oblige a state to refuse its own nationals entry into its territory;

(f) in order to ensure compliance with the requirements of this paragraph, and thereby preventing illicit trafficking in nuclear, chemical or biological weapons, their means of delivery and related materials, all Member States are called upon to take, in accor-

A police officer walks past North and South Korean missiles at the Korea War Memorial Museum after North Korea agreed to shut down its nuclear reactor and dismantle its atomic weapons program.

dance with their national authorities and legislation, and consistent with international law, cooperative action including thorough inspection of cargo to and from the DPRK, as necessary; . . .

North Korea Must Be Controlled

14. *Calls upon* the DPRK to return immediately to the Six-Party Talks without precondition and to work towards the expeditious implementation of the Joint Statement issued on 19 September 2005 by China, the DPRK, Japan, the Republic of Korea, the Russian Federation and the United States;

15. *Affirms* that it shall keep DPRK's actions under continuous review and that it shall be prepared to review the appropriateness of the measures contained in paragraph 8 above, including the strengthening, modification, suspension or lifting of the measures, as may be needed at that time in light of the DPRK's compliance with the provisions of the resolution;

16. *Underlines* that further decisions will be required, should additional measures be necessary;

17. *Decides* to remain actively seized of the matter.

EVALUATING THE AUTHORS' ARGUMENTS:

The purpose of the sanctions imposed against North Korea is to punish North Korea for violating international law, to prevent it from further developing its weapons program, and to weaken the North Korean leadership. The author of the following viewpoint, Nicholas D. Kristof, argues that such sanctions will not accomplish these goals. How effective do you think sanctions can be? Do they adequately pressure a rogue nation and weaken it? If yes, explain your reasoning. If no, suggest another way rogue nations might be dealt with if they break international law.

Sanctions Will Not Force North Korea to Give Up Its Weapons of Mass Destruction

"The biggest threat to North Korea's regime isn't from American warships, but from the sight of other Koreans dieting, or listening on iPods to love songs, or watching decadent television comedies."

Nicholas D. Kristof

In the following viewpoint author Nicholas D. Kristof argues that imposing sanctions on North Korea will only harden leader Kim Jong-Il's grip on his people. Because sanctions are intended to isolate a nation, North Koreans have little idea of what the rest of the world is like. Thus, argues Kristof, they are forced to rely on the North Korean leadership for everything. This arrangement helps solidify Kim Jong-Il's regime. Kristof suggests that if North Koreans knew about the luxuries and freedoms the outside world has to offer, they would not give Kim Jong-Il the support he needs to remain in power. For these reasons, Kristof argues against imposing sanctions in order to undermine North Korean leadership.

Nicholas D. Kristof is a columnist for the *New York Times*, from which this viewpoint is taken.

AS YOU READ, CONSIDER THE FOLLOWING QUESTIONS:
1. According to Kristof, what four nations does the United States despise, and what do they have in common?
2. In what way do sanctions preserve the North Korean regime's authority, according to the author?
3. What could pose the biggest threat to Kim Jong-Il's authority, in Kristof's opinion?

A North Korean visiting South Korea once sniffed that all the cars must have been brought in from around the country just to make a good impression for his visit. His South Korean host added dryly that it had been even more difficult to bring in all the tall buildings.

Such interactions with the outside world are the best hope to chip away at North Korean totalitarianism but we've missed the opportunity because for decades we've conspired with Kim Jong-Il to isolate his people.

Who Is to Blame for a Nuclear North Korea?

Lately Americans have been quarreling over who is more to blame for North Korea's nuclear test, [former president] Bill Clinton or George W. Bush.

Well, Mr. Clinton inherited a situation that, if it had continued, would have resulted in North Korea having hundreds of nuclear weapons by now, and producing an additional 50 each year. Instead, Mr. Clinton negotiated a deal with North Korea that resulted in it producing not a single ounce of new plutonium in his eight years in office.

In contrast, President Bush inherited that North Korean nuclear freeze and, if he had just left it alone, North Korea wouldn't have produced any new plutonium. But

FAST FACT

UN Resolution 1718 banned the sale of luxury items to North Korea, which includes items such as automobiles, liquor, cigarettes, melons, beef, and home electronic goods.

The international community has no business imposing punitive sanctions on the people of North Korea...

That's MY job...

KIM JONG IL

KIM JONG IL

MARGULIES
©2006 THE RECORD NEW JERSEY
www.northjersey.com/margulies

Mr. Bush overruled [former secretary of state] Colin Powell's efforts to continue the engagement—and so North Korea has churned out enough plutonium on Mr. Bush's watch for perhaps eight nuclear weapons.

But in a larger sense, the North Korean nuclear test—and the fact that Kim Jong-Il is still in power—represent a failure not so much of either Mr. Bush or Mr. Clinton, but of decades of bipartisan American policy that aimed to isolate the North.

Sanctions Help North Korea

Look around the world at the regimes we despise: North Korea, Cuba, Burma and Iran. Those are among the world's most long-lived regimes, and that's partly because the sanctions and isolation we have imposed on them have actually propped them up—by giving those countries' leaders an excuse for their economic failures and a chance to cloak themselves in nationalism.

Kim Jong-Il sees that the best way to preserve North Korean total-itarianism is in the formaldehyde of its own isolation. In effect, Mr. Kim has placed sanctions on his own country, and we're abetting him.

In the 1970's, North Korea poked its head out of its shell, negotiating with South Korea, seeking foreign investors and sending letters to [then President] Jimmy Carter seeking talks. Mr. Carter considered inviting the leaders of North and South Korea to a summit meeting at a place like Camp David—but dropped the idea when his own aides reacted with horror.

Yet if we had held such a meeting, and gradually encouraged trade and other contacts, North Korea's regime might well have collapsed by now. At least, it would have moderated enough that the country would look like China or Vietnam.

Sanctions Don't Work

I lived in China in the 1980's and 1990's when Communist ideology was collapsing there, and I'm convinced that the best way to undermine North Korea's government would be to send in business executives—overweight ones, if possible. In a country like North Korea, where the government responded to famine by broadcasting a cautionary

A U.S. army soldier prepares for a chemical attack drill that will help him learn how to respond in the event that North Korea uses its stockpile of chemical weapons.

"documentary" about a man who exploded after eating too much rice, nothing would be more subversive than tubby foreigners.

Mr. Bush is right that we have to punish North Korea for its brazen nuclear test, and the administration has been sensible and prudent . . . in devising a series of penalties. But after North Korea drags itself back to six-party talks, we should begin to move away from our long, failed strategy of trying to isolate the world's most isolated country.

In particular, it's a mistake for us to reproach the South Koreans—who have more of a stake than anybody, and who understand the North Koreans better than we do—for operating factories in the Kaesong industrial zone in North Korea.

Exposure to the World Will Undermine North Korea

It's true that those North Korean workers have no rights, and that North Korea will use the hard currency to bolster its military. But those South Korean factories are expected to employ 700,000 workers by 2012.

While North Korea can survive punitive sanctions, I don't think the regime can survive the shock of having 700,000 of its citizens working for South Korean capitalists—and realizing that the southerners are so rich and spoiled that they refuse to eat rice with gravel in it.

The biggest threat to North Korea's regime isn't from American warships, but from the sight of other Koreans dieting, or listening on iPods to love songs, or watching decadent television comedies.

So let's stop helping the Dear Leader isolate his own people.

EVALUATING THE AUTHOR'S ARGUMENTS:

Nicholas D. Kristof argues that material objects such as iPods, fancy cars, and good food can destabilize the North Korean regime more than sanctions can. Clarify what he means by this. Do you think he is right? Explain your answer thoroughly.

Diplomacy Will Force North Korea to Give Up Its Weapons of Mass Destruction

Robert L. Gallucci

"It may be righteous, denying North Korea the reward of bilateral talks, but it has failed to secure U.S. interests."

In the following viewpoint author Robert L. Gallucci argues that diplomacy is the only option for diffusing the nuclear threat from North Korea. Since diplomatic talks were ended under the George W. Bush administration, North Korea's nuclear abilities have grown—in October 2006 it became the ninth nuclear power in the world. Gallucci argues that neither military options nor sanctions can adequately counter the very real threat from a nuclear North Korea. He therefore urges the United States and other nations to resume talks with North Korea—such talks have the best chance of disarming the rogue regime, he concludes.

Robert L. Gallucci is dean of the School of Foreign Service at Georgetown University. He has authored a number of publications on political-military issues, including *Neither Peace nor Honor: The Politics of American Military Policy in Vietnam.*

AS YOU READ, CONSIDER THE FOLLOWING QUESTIONS:
1. As reported by the author, what progress did North Korea make on its nuclear weapons program in the 1980s?
2. Why is military action against North Korea not a viable option in the author's opinion?
3. What does the word *vexing* mean in the context of the viewpoint?

The political consequences of the North Korean nuclear test are likely to be severe, domestically and internationally. Eventually in Seoul and Tokyo there will be serious discussion of the virtue of continued nuclear abstinence. And the North undoubtedly learned something from its test, so it is one step closer to mating nuclear weapons to an extended-range ballistic missile capable of hitting Tokyo today and Los Angeles tomorrow. Most ominous of all, as we and our friends in the U.N. Security Council passed the toughest sanctions resolution we can—as we must, at least to set an example for others—we push the North Koreans ever closer to crossing the ultimate red line: selling fissile material to al-Qaeda. That poses a threat against which our country has no real defense and no effective deterrent. It is the most serious threat to our national security.

While some have reduced a critical and complex foreign policy issue to a debating point in partisan politics, it is important to sort out the facts of what has happened in the past decade or so if we want to chart a more effective course for policy.

North Korea's Nuclear History

North Korea began building its nuclear-weapons program in the 1980s, just as it was signing the Nuclear Nonproliferation Treaty. By the time President Bill Clinton was sworn into office, Pyongyang had already separated enough plutonium for one or two nuclear weapons. The President was told by his intelligence community that if the North

North Korea's Nuclear Timeline

Mid-1980s: First signs of North Korea's nuclear program are detected by U.S. intelligence.

1986: North Korea produces plutonium in reactor.

1991: U.S. begins talks with North Korea to end their nuclear program.

1992: North Korea separates enough weapons-grade plutonium to make one or two bombs.

1993: North Korea announces it will leave Nuclear Non-Proliferation Treaty.

1994: Clinton administration proposes the Framework Agreement, which results in North Korea freezing nuclear production for the next eight years.

1998: North Korea tests medium-range "Taep'o-dong-1" missile.

1999: Pyongyang agrees to a moratorium on its long-range missile program.

2001: President George W. Bush slows negotiations with North Korea.

2002: Bush labels North Korea a member of the "Axis of Evil."

March 2003: United States invades Iraq.

April 2003: North Korea withdraws from the Nuclear Non-Proliferation Treaty; soon thereafter, they restart their reactor.

April 2005: North Korea appears to unload nuclear reactor with up to 15 kg of weapons-grade plutonium.

September 19, 2005: In six-party talks, North Korea agrees to abandon its nuclear program in exchange for an incentives package.

September 19, 2005: U.S. places sanctions on the bank that provides financial support for North Korean government agencies; causes collapse of the September 2005 agreement.

June 2006: North Korea is believed to have produced enough plutonium for four to thirteen nuclear bombs.

July 2006: North Korea tests missiles: one medium-range and five short-range. Medium-range "Taep'o-dong-2" fails.

October 9, 2006: North Korea tests an atomic weapon; officially becomes the ninth nuclear power.

October 14, 2006: The UN votes to impose sanctions against North Korea.

Korean program was not stopped, the existing reactor and two others under construction would produce, within approximately five years, enough plutonium to manufacture 30 nuclear weapons annually. In close consultation with our allies in Seoul and Tokyo, the President authorized direct bilateral negotiations. Sixteen difficult months later, with the U.S. military presence on the Korean peninsula visibly enhanced and the threat of U.N. sanctions looming, the Agreed Framework was concluded. It clearly provided for the immediate freezing of the entire North Korean nuclear program and its eventual dismantlement—as well as the resolution of the vexing problem of the plutonium produced before Clinton took office.

This history is pretty clear, but what happens next, less so. The North complied with its obligations to freeze its nuclear program but later began to cheat by secretly receiving components for a gas-centrifuge uranium-enrichment facility from Pakistan. The Clinton Administration planned to take up the matter with the North, but time ran out.

A Failed Policy

When President George W. Bush came into office, he, like Clinton, was confronted with a situation in North Korea—but one that was far less pressing: the plutonium for one or two nuclear weapons was still somewhere in North Korea, but no more had been separated. The entire plutonium-production program was frozen and under International Atomic Energy Agency inspection; and the other elements of the framework were on track. The problem was the secret North Korean effort to enrich uranium for a nuclear-weapons program. The Bush Administration's approach to the problem quickly took shape when it confronted Pyongyang with the knowledge of the secret program and the demand that the North give it up before any further negotiations could take place. When Pyongyang

FAST FACT

Diplomacy successfully convinced Libya to dismantle its weapons of mass destruction programs on December 19, 2003. Libya was once regarded as a dangerous nation that supported terrorism.

South Korean and North Korean delegates begin talks aimed at reducing tension along their borders.

refused, the U.S. abandoned the Agreed Framework, prompting North Korea to do likewise—kicking inspectors out, starting up the reactor, separating plutonium and announcing the acquisition of a deterrent.

What are we to make of this brief history? It is difficult to see how the current situation can be said to have resulted from the Clinton policy of engagement. Indeed, what has the current policy, which is far more resistant to negotiating, gained us? It may be righteous, denying North Korea the reward of bilateral talks, but it has failed to secure U.S. interests.

Diplomacy Is the Only Real Option

There are now—and have always been—only three options available to deal with the North Korean problem: military force, sanctions and negotiation. Although the military option was available but unappealing a dozen years ago, it is barely so today. Limited targets, little reserve force to deal with retaliation and an ally in Seoul hostile to military action argue against that option. Sanctions, always limited by what China would permit, will not force North Korean compliance and amount to a policy of containment or acceptance of a growing North Korean nuclear-weapons program. That poses unacceptable risks to our nation's security.

That leaves negotiation—genuine negotiation in which we expect to get what we need and concede to the North at least some of what it wants. Our objective should be to focus on the country's nuclear program, insisting on its complete dismantlement and a full accounting of fissile material. We must be prepared to meet Pyongyang's concerns too—security assurances, energy assistance (including those proliferation-resistant nuclear reactors) and eventual normalization of relations. And there must always be an "or else"—that is, we must persuade Seoul, Tokyo and Beijing to support even more painful sanctions if necessary in the future so that the North is properly motivated. That is by far the best course, and we had better get on with it.

EVALUATING THE AUTHOR'S ARGUMENTS:

In the viewpoint you just read, Robert L. Gallucci uses history, facts, and examples to make his argument that diplomacy is the only option for defusing the nuclear threat from North Korea. He does not, however, use any quotations to support his point. If you were to rewrite this article and insert quotations, what authorities might you quote from? Where would you place these quotations to bolster the points Gallucci makes?

Bribery Will Force North Korea to Give Up Its Weapons of Mass Destruction

"Kim would probably relinquish his nuclear weapons if he were offered enough food and oil aid, an end to trade embargoes, and a firm U.S. promise not to try to overthrow him."

Gwynne Dyer

In the following viewpoint author Gwynne Dyer argues that the international community should give North Korea food, oil, and other commodities it needs in exchange for relinquishing its nuclear weapons. North Korea has always tried to blackmail the world for these items, she explains. In fact, its whole desire for nuclear weapons is an elaborate game of blackmail for these items. Dyer argues the United States should simply give North Korea such materials in exchange for relinquishing nuclear weapons —it is a much cheaper and effective solution than imposing sanctions or going to war.

Gwynne Dyer is a London-based independent journalist whose articles are published in newspapers in forty-five countries, including the *Athens (OH) News*, from which this viewpoint was taken.

AS YOU READ, CONSIDER THE FOLLOWING QUESTIONS:
1. Why does the author view North Korea's acquisition of nuclear weapons as "a cry for help?"
2. Describe the terms of the 1994 Framework Agreement as relayed by the author.
3. Why does the author believe sanctions should not be pursued against North Korea?

In psychobabble, what North Korea has just done [by conducting a nuclear test over world objections] would be best characterized as "a cry for help," like a teenage kid burning his parents' house down because he's misunderstood. Granted, it's an unusually loud cry for help, but now that North Korean dictator Kim Jong-Il has got our attention, what are we going to do about him?

North Korea's nuclear-weapon test early Monday morning [on October 9, 2006] makes it the ninth nuclear power, and by far the least predictable. It probably has only a few nuclear weapons, and it certainly cannot deliver them to any targets beyond South Korea and Japan, but the notion of nuclear weapons in the hands of a "crazy state" frightens people.

So relax: Kim Jong-Il is not crazy. Former US Secretary of State Madeleine Albright, who has negotiated with him, says he is well informed and not at all delusional. He pretends to be unstable because his regime's survival depends on blackmailing foreign countries into giving it the food and fuel that it cannot produce for itself. Rogue nukes are a big part of that image, but like any professional black-mailer, he would hand them over for the right price.

Blackmailing the World

Put yourself in Kim's (platform) shoes. In 1994 he inherited a country from his father, Kim Il-Sung, that was already in acute crisis. The centralized Stalinist economy had been failing for a decade, and in 1991 post-Soviet Russia cut off the flow of subsidized oil, fertilizer and food, effectively halving North Korea's Gross Domestic Product.

Yet Kim needed the support of the military and the Party officials who controlled North Korea's "command" economy and derived their power and privileges from it. Radical economic reforms would threaten their positions. Kim's inheritance was far from secure, so he left the economy alone and used the threat of going nuclear to extort aid from foreign countries.

The younger Kim had been put in charge of North Korea's nuclear weapons program by his father in the late '80s. By 1993, Washington was so concerned that it offered Pyongyang a deal: stop the program, and the U.S. would give North Korea huge amounts of foreign aid. Kim Il-Sung died in July, 1994, and it was his son who approved the "Framework Agreement" with the United States that October in which the U.S. promised to send Pyongyang half a million tons of oil a year and to eventually build the North Koreans two nuclear reactors.

China, South Korea and other neighbours chipped in, sending grain, other food and medicines. Kim Jong-Il won some breathing space to consolidate his rule—but then a series of floods and droughts overwhelmed the country's inefficient collective farms, and up to a million North Koreans starved. By 2002, in desperation, Kim Jong-Il played the nuclear card again.

FAST FACT

For more than a decade, North Koreans have suffered from famine and acute food shortages. Hundreds of thousands have died of starvation, and millions have suffered from chronic malnutrition.

An Ongoing Nuclear Desire

American intelligence picked up the renewed nuclear activity, and in October 2002 the North Koreans admitted to U.S. Assistant Secretary of State James Kelly that they had a secret nuclear weapons program in defiance of the 1994 Agreed Framework. (Blackmail only works if the target is aware of the threat.)

American Opinions on North Korea

A 2006 poll found that Americans hold the following opinions about North Korea:*

Do you think North Korea poses a real national security threat to the United States?

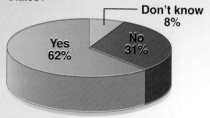

Don't know 8%
No 31%
Yes 62%

Do you think Iran poses a real national security threat to the United States?

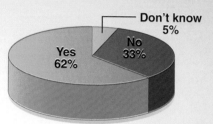

Don't know 5%
No 33%
Yes 62%

Do you think the situation in Iraq has led the United States to be less aggressive with North Korea and Iran than it should be?

Don't know 10%
No 37%
Yes 54%

Do you think a toughly worded resolution from the United Nations will help a lot toward preventing North Korea from continuing to develop its weapons program, help some, or not help at all?

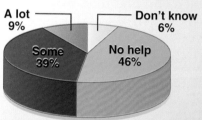

A lot 9%
Don't know 6%
Some 39%
No help 46%

Do you think North Korea is deliberately trying to provoke war, or is it just trying to get attention to get more money and aid from the United States and other countries?

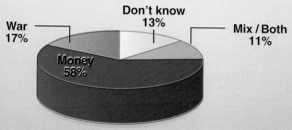

War 17%
Don't know 13%
Mix / Both 11%
Money 58%

* Figures are approximate.

Source: Fox News/Opinion Dynamics Poll, July 13, 2006.

This time, the U.S. refused to yield to blackmail, so the past four years have seen North Korea withdraw from the Nuclear Non-Proliferation Treaty, throw out International Atomic Energy Agency inspectors, test-fire missiles near South Korea and Japan on several occasions, and now test an actual nuclear weapon. Kim Jong-Il only has one card, and he keeps trying to play it.

Kim's crude tactics were always intensely irritating to the other parties to the Six-Power Talks on North Korea's nuclear weapons (the U.S., Russia, China, Japan and South Korea), and now they are furious with the little dictator. Even China, North Korea's only ally, called Pyongyang's test "stupid." But what are they actually going to do about it?

Sanctions, I hear you cry. But the U.S. has had sanctions against North Korea since 1953, and Japan has had them for more than a decade already—and if China stops sending aid, the economy will collapse, millions will starve, and millions more will flee the country. I was at the Foreign Ministry in Seoul in 1994 on the day that Kim Il-sung died, and I remember the panic that reigned as South Korea's diplomatic elite contemplated the prospect of 25 million starving North Koreans suddenly landing in their laps.

It has been suggested that providing North Korea with food and oil would be more effective than a military approach in ending their nuclear weapons program.

Stop the Nonsense

The regime in Beijing is equally appalled at the notion of millions of North Korean refugees pouring across its border, so there may be sanctions, but they will not be life threatening for Pyongyang. Which brings us back to the distasteful business of bargaining with black-mailers.

Kim would probably relinquish his nuclear weapons if he were offered enough food and oil aid, an end to trade embargoes, and a firm U.S. promise not to try to overthrow him. None of that would cost very much, and the U.S. is not going to attack him anyway. Nor has Kim any intention of attacking anybody, especially with nuclear weapons: he would have no hope of surviving the instant and crushing retaliation by American nuclear weapons. So it's just a question of persuading him to stop the nonsense.

But what about the principle of the thing? Won't other countries be tempted to follow North Korea's example if we don't punish it for developing nuclear weapons? You know, like we did when Israel, India and Pakistan developed theirs.

EVALUATING THE AUTHOR'S ARGUMENTS:

Gwynne Dyer explains that North Korea's desire for nuclear weapons stems from a desire to blackmail the rest of the world for things it needs. She suggests giving in to this blackmail could be a way to eliminate North Korea's nuclear program. What do you think? Could giving North Korea the goods it wants solve the problem or create another one? Explain your answer using evidence from the texts you have read.

Facts About Weapons of Mass Destruction

Weapons of Mass Destruction and Iraq

- The United States supplied Iraq with biological and chemical weapons when the two countries were allies in the 1980s.
- According to the Senate committee's reports titled "U.S. Chemical and Biological Warfare-Related Dual-Use Exports to Iraq":
  - In May 1986 two batches of *Bacillus anthracis*—the microorganism that causes anthrax—were shipped to the Iraqi Ministry of Higher Education, along with two batches of the bacterium *Clostridium botulinum*, the agent that causes deadly botulism poisoning.
  - A batch of salmonella and *E. coli* were shipped to the Iraqi State Company for Drug Industries on August 31, 1987.
  - The Ronald Reagan and George H.W. Bush administrations sold anthrax, VX nerve gas, West Nile fever germs, and botulism, as well as germs similar to tuberculosis and pneumonia, to Iraq through March 1992.
  - Other bacteria sold included *Brucella melitensis*, which damages major organs, and *Clostridium perfringens*, which causes gas gangrene.
  - Britain sold Iraq the drug pralidoxine, an antidote to nerve gas, in March 1992, after the end of the Gulf War. Pralidoxine can be reverse engineered to create nerve gas.
- According to the former UN chief weapons inspector in Iraq, Scott Ritter, between 90 percent and 95 percent of Iraq's weapons of mass destruction were destroyed by the UN in the 1990s, while the remainder were probably used or destroyed during the first Gulf War.
- The Iraq War of 2003 was fought largely because the United States claimed dictator Saddam Hussein was pursuing weapons of mass destruction programs.
- Though a few hundred missiles and mustard gas agents were found in the aftermath of the 2003 Iraq War, their condition was

such that they could not be used to cause any real damage. Therefore the majority of voices, including key members of the Bush administration, concede that as of December 2006 no weapons of mass destruction such as the kind that were claimed to be there prior to the war have been found.

Weapons of Mass Destruction and North Korea

- North Korea was a member of the Nuclear Non-Proliferation Treaty but withdrew in 2003.
- In 2003 President George W. Bush named North Korea as part of an "axis of evil" due to its determination to obtain nuclear weapons. The other two members of the axis of evil were Iraq and Iran.
- On October 9, 2006, the North Korean government successfully conducted a nuclear test for the first time.
- Both the U.S. Geologic Survey and Japanese seismological authorities detected the equivalent of a 4.2 magnitude earthquake in North Korea, indicating a small bomb had in fact been detonated.
- On October 14, 2006, the UN Security Council passed a resolution imposing sanctions on North Korea for its October 9, 2006, nuclear test.
- North Korea is widely believed to possess a substantial arsenal of other weapons of mass destruction. It reportedly acquired the technology necessary to produce tabun and mustard gas as early as the 1950s, and it now possesses a full arsenal of nerve agents and other advanced varieties and has developed the means to launch them in artillery shells.
- North Korea has a large artillery arsenal within range of Seoul, South Korea, and several cities in eastern China.

Weapons of Mass Destruction and the United States

According to the Natural Resources Defense Council's *Nuclear Notebook*, the CIA, the Defense Intelligence Agency, and the Pentagon:
- As of 2006 the United States had a total of 9,962 nuclear weapons stationed in locations within the United States and around the world. This includes 5,735 active or operational warheads: 5,235 strategic and 500 nonstrategic warheads.

- Approximately 4,225 additional warheads are held in the reserve or inactive stockpiles, some of which will be dismantled. Some 4,365 warheads are scheduled to be retired for dismantlement by 2012.
- Since 1997 the Pentagon has removed nuclear weapons from three states (California, Virginia, and South Dakota), and the size of its nuclear stockpile has decreased from about 12,500 warheads to just fewer than 10,000.
- In 1991 the United States withdrew all of its nuclear weapons from South Korea, and thousands more from Europe by 1993.
- The army and Marine Corps denuclearized in the early 1990s, and in 1992 the navy swiftly off-loaded all nuclear weapons from aircraft carriers and other surface vessels.
- By 1994 the navy had eliminated these ships' nuclear capability, and many air force, navy, and army bases and storage depots closed overseas as a result.
- Today, perhaps as many as four hundred bombs remain at eight facilities in six European countries, the last remnant of the Cold War era. Nuclear warheads remain in Belgium, Germany, Italy, Netherlands, Turkey, and Britain.
- Nuclear warheads have been removed from Alaska, Canada, Chichi-Jima, Cuba, France, Greece, Greenland, Guam, Hawaii, Iwo Jima, Japan, Johnston Island, Kwajalein Atoll, Midway Islands, Morocco, Okinawa, Philippines, Puerto Rico, South Korea, Spain, and Taiwan.
- Despite dismantlements and retirings, the United States continues to spend billions of dollars annually to maintain and upgrade its nuclear forces.
- Of the more than seventy thousand warheads produced by the United States since 1945, more than sixty thousand have been disassembled as of late 2006.
- The United States is responsible for building about 97 percent of the total nuclear weapons ever to have been built.

Weapons of Mass Destruction Around the World

- The United States is the only country ever to have dropped nuclear weapons in wartime. It dropped two atomic bombs on the Japanese cities of Hiroshima and Nagasaki at the end of World War II, killing as many as 214,000 people.

- More than 128,000 nuclear warheads have been built worldwide since 1945.
- The total global nuclear weapons stockpile has been reduced from the 1986 Cold War high of 70,000-plus warheads to about 27,000 warheads, its lowest level in forty-five years.
- About 12,500 of these warheads are considered operational, with the rest in reserve or retired and awaiting dismantlement.
- In the same period, the number of nuclear weapon states has grown from five to nine—the United States, France, China, Great Britain, Russia, India, Pakistan, North Korea, and unofficially Israel.
- Ninety-seven percent of the world's nuclear weapons are in U.S. and Russian stockpiles.
- India and Pakistan have an estimated 110 nuclear warheads altogether, but neither have released any official information to the public about the size of their arsenals.
- North Korea is estimated to have as many as ten nuclear weapons.
- Though Israel has not acknowledged it possesses nuclear weapons, the Defense Intelligence Agency estimates it has between sixty and eighty-five warheads.
- Russia is estimated to have about 5,830 operational nuclear weapons.
- Britain is estimated to have about 200 operational nuclear weapons.
- The French nuclear stockpile includes approximately 350 warheads, down from 540 in 1992.
- China is estimated to have a nuclear arsenal of about 200 nuclear warheads, down from an estimated 435 in 1993.
- U.S. intelligence has projected that Iran is about a decade away from manufacturing the key ingredient for a nuclear weapon, unless it purchases it from a rogue nation such as North Korea before then.

Facts About the Nuclear Non-Proliferation Treaty

- The Nuclear Non-Proliferation Treaty went into effect in 1970.
- It stipulates that the only countries allowed to have nuclear

weapons are the five that possessed them at the time the treaty was written: the United States, France, China, Great Britain, and the former Soviet Union, now Russia.

- Since then, four additional countries have acquired nuclear weapons: India (1998), Pakistan (1998), and North Korea (2006); Israel has not admitted to having nuclear weapons, but it is widely agreed it does.
- One hundred eighty-eight countries have signed the Nuclear Non-Proliferation Treaty, vowing not to pursue nuclear weapons.

Glossary

Al Qaeda: Osama bin Laden's international terrorist group that was responsible for the September 11, 2001, terrorist attacks on the United States.

anthrax: An infectious disease contracted from animals that is often fatal. Used as a bioweapon in 2001 in the United States.

asymmetric threat: The use of crude or low-tech weapons to attack a superior or high-tech enemy.

axis of evil: The triple threat of Iran, Iraq, and North Korea mentioned by President George W. Bush during his State of the Union speech in 2002.

biological warfare: The intentional use of viruses, bacteria, other microorganisms, or toxins derived from living organisms to cause death or disease in humans, animals, or plants.

botulism: A disease caused by a naturally occurring toxin called botulinum that is lethal and simple to produce. Food supply contamination or aerosol dissemination of the botulinum toxin are two ways it could be used by terrorists.

chemical attack: The intentional release of toxic liquid, gas, or solids.

chemical weapons: Weapons that harm living targets, such as sarin, VX nerve gas, or mustard gas.

Department of Homeland Security (DHS): A new department charged with protecting the United States, created after the September 11 terrorist attacks.

dirty bomb: A makeshift nuclear device that is created from radioactive nuclear waste material.

Federal Emergency Management Agency (FEMA): An agency charged with responding to, planning for, recovering from, and protecting against natural and man-made disasters.

germ warfare: The use of biological agents to inflict damage or death on people, animals, or plants.

Hamas: The Islamic Resistance Movement, tied to the Muslim Brotherhood, calling for the creation of an Islamic state in all of historic Palestine. Hamas has a military wing that conducts terrorist acts on Israeli civilians and a political wing that was elected to power in January 2006.

highly enriched uranium (HEU): Uranium that is technologically enhanced to be used in nuclear weapons and in some types of research and submarine propulsion reactors.

mustard gas: A chemical weapon that causes severe damage to the eyes, internal organs, and respiratory system. It was first used in combat in World War I. Victims suffer the effects of mustard gas thirty or forty years after exposure.

nerve agents: Insecticides that have been developed into chemical weapons. Includes VX, sarin, soman, and tabun. Only a small quantity is needed to inflict substantial damage.

nuclear detonation: An explosion resulting from fission and/or fusion reactions in nuclear material, such as that from a nuclear weapon.

plague: The pneumonic plague, which could be used by terrorists in biowarfare, is naturally carried by rodents and fleas but can be aerosolized and sprayed from crop dusters. The World Health Organization estimates that a dissemination of 110 pounds (50kg) in an aerosol cloud over a city of 5 million could result in 150,000 cases of pneumonic plague, 80,000 to 100,000 of which would require hospitalization, and 36,000 of which would be expected to die.

preparedness: All measures taken before an event occurs that allow for prevention and readiness. Preparedness includes designing warning systems, planning for evacuation and relocation, storing food and water, building temporary shelter, devising management strategies, and holding disaster drills and exercises.

radiological dispersal device: An explosive device that is intended to spread radioactive material from the detonation of conventional explosives.

sarin: A colorless, odorless, lethal gas. Sarin degrades quickly in humid weather, but sarin's life expectancy increases as the temperature gets higher, regardless of how humid it is.

stockpile: An area or storehouse where medicine and other supplies are kept in the event of an emergency.

weapons of mass destruction (WMD): The National Defense Authorization Act defines WMDs as "any weapon or device that is intended, or has the capability, to cause death or serious bodily injury to a significant number of people through the release, dissemination, or impact of (A) toxic or poisonous chemicals or their precursors; (B) a disease organism; or (C) radiation or radioactivity."

Organizations to Contact

The editors have compiled the following list of organizations concerned with the issues debated in this book. The descriptions are derived from materials provided by the organizations. All have publications or information available for interested readers. The list was compiled on the date of publication of the present volume; the information provided here may change. Be aware that many organizations take several weeks or longer to respond to inquiries, so allow as much time as possible.

The American Civil Defense Association (TACDA)
11576 S. State St., Suite 502
Draper, UT 84020
(800) 425-5397
fax: (904) 964-9641
e-mail: defense@tacda.org
Web site: www.tacda.org

TACDA was established in the early 1960s in an effort to help promote civil defense awareness and disaster preparedness, both in the military and the private sector, and to assist citizens in their efforts to prepare for all types of natural and man-made disasters. Publications include the quarterly *Journal of Civil Defense* and the *TACDA Alert* newsletter.

American Enterprise Institute (AEI)
1150 Seventeenth St. NW
Washington, DC 20036
(202) 862-5800
fax: (202) 862-7177
Web site: www.aei.org

The American Enterprise Institute for Public Policy Research is a scholarly research institute that is dedicated to preserving limited government, private enterprise, and a strong foreign policy and national defense.

AEI publishes books including *The End of North Korea*; its magazine, *American Enterprise*, often deals with developments in Korea and Asia.

America's Future
7800 Bonhomme Ave.
St. Louis, MO 63105
(314) 725-6003
fax: (314) 721-3373
e-mail: info@americasfuture.net
Web site: www.americasfuture.net

America's Future seeks to educate the public about the importance of the principles upon which the U.S. government is founded and on the value of the free enterprise system. It supports continued U.S. testing of nuclear weapons and their usefulness as a deterrent of war. The group publishes the monthly newsletter *America's Future*.

Arms Control Association (ACA)
1150 Connecticut Ave. NW, Suite 620
Washington, DC 20036
(202) 463-8270
fax: (202) 463-8273
e-mail: aca@armscontrol.org
Web site: www.armscontrol.org

The Arms Control Association is a nonprofit organization dedicated to promoting public understanding of and support for effective arms control policies. ACA seeks to increase public appreciation of the need to limit arms, reduce international tensions, and promote world peace. It publishes the monthly magazine *Arms Control Today*.

Carnegie Endowment for International Peace
1779 Massachusetts Ave. NW
Washington, DC 20036
(202) 483-7600
fax: (202) 483-1840
e-mail: info@ceip.org
Web site: www.ceip.org

The Carnegie Endowment for International Peace conducts research on international affairs and U.S. foreign policy. Issues concerning nuclear weapons and proliferation are often discussed in articles published in its quarterly journal, *Foreign Policy.*

Center for Defense Information (CDI)
1779 Massachusetts Ave. NW, Suite 615
Washington, DC 20036
(202) 332-0600
fax: (202) 462-4559
e-mail: info@cdi.org
Web site: www.cdi.org

CDI is composed of civilians and former military officers who oppose both excessive expenditures for weapons and policies that increase the danger of war. The center serves as an independent monitor of the military, analyzing spending, policies, weapon systems, and related military issues. It publishes the *Defense Monitor* ten times per year.

Center for Nonproliferation Studies
460 Pierce St.
Monterey, CA 93940
(831) 647-4154
fax: (831) 647-3519
E-mail: cns@miis.edu
Web site: http://cns.miis.edu

The center researches all aspects of nonproliferation and works to combat the spread of weapons of mass destruction. The center produces research databases and has multiple reports, papers, speeches, and congressional testimony available online. Its main publication is the *Nonproliferation Review*, which is published three times per year.

Federation of American Scientists
1717 K St. NW, Suite 209
Washington, DC 20036
(202) 546-3300
Web site: www.fas.org

The Federation of American Scientists was formed in 1945 by atomic scientists from the Manhattan Project who felt that scientists, engineers, and other innovators had an ethical obligation to bring their knowledge and experience to bear on critical national decisions, especially pertaining to the technology they had unleashed—the atomic bomb. Its Web site contains numerous reports on issues related to weapons of mass destruction.

Henry L. Stimson Center
1111 Nineteenth St., 12th Fl.
Washington, DC 20036
(202) 223-5956
E-mail: info@stimson.org
Web site: www.stimson.org

The Stimson Center is an independent, nonprofit public policy institute committed to finding and promoting innovative solutions to the security challenges confronting the United States and other nations. The center directs the Chemical and Biological Weapons Non-proliferation Project, which serves as a clearinghouse of information related to the monitoring and implementation of the 1993 Chemical Weapons Convention. The center produces occasional papers, reports, handbooks, and books on chemical and biological weapons policy, nuclear policy, and eliminating weapons of mass destruction.

Korean Peninsula Energy Development Organization (KEDO)
Public and External Promotion and Support Division
600 Third Ave., 12th Fl.
New York, NY 10016
(212) 455-0200
fax: (212) 681-2647
Web site: www.kedo.org

KEDO is an international nonprofit organization established to carry out key provisions of the Agreed Framework negotiated in 1994 between the United States and North Korea in which North Korea promised to freeze its nuclear facilities development. The organization works to help North Korea build civilian nuclear reactors and provide other energy sources to that nation. Its Web site includes reports and press releases on its activities.

Nuclear Age Peace Foundation
1187 Coast Village Rd., Suite 1, PMB 121
Santa Barbara, California 93108-2794

(805) 965-3443
fax: (805) 568-0466
Web site: www.wagingpeace.org

Founded in 1982, the Nuclear Age Peace Foundation, a nonprofit, non-partisan, international education and advocacy organization, initiates and supports worldwide efforts to abolish nuclear weapons, to strengthen international law and institutions, to use technology responsibly and sustainably, and to empower youth to create a more peaceful world. Its Web site, WagingPeace.org, has a searchable database of news, editorials, and articles, including "Terrorism and Nonviolence" and "The Iraq War and the Future of International Law."

Peace Action
1100 Wayne Ave., Suite 1020
Silver Spring, MD 20910
(301) 565-4050
e-mail: paprog@igc.org
Web site: www.peace-action.org

Peace Action is a grassroots peace and justice organization that works for policy changes in Congress and the United Nations, as well as state and city legislatures. The national office houses an organizing department that promotes education and activism on topics related to peace and disarmament issues. The organization produces a quarterly newsletter and also publishes an annual voting record for members of Congress.

Project Ploughshares
57 Erb St. West
Waterloo, ON
Canada N2L 6C2
(519) 888-6541
fax: (519) 888-0018
e-mail: plough@ploughshares.ca
Web site: www.ploughshares.ca

Project Ploughshares promotes disarmament and demilitarization, the peaceful resolution of political conflict, and the pursuit of security based on equity, justice, and a sustainable environment. Public understanding and support for these goals is encouraged through research, education, and development of constructive policy alternatives.

Union of Concerned Scientists (UCS)
2 Brattle Sq.
Cambridge, MA 02238
(617) 547-5552
fax: (617) 864-9405
e-mail: ucs@ucsusa.org
Web site: www.ucsusa.org

UCS is concerned about the impact of advanced technology on society. It supports nuclear arms control as a means to reduce nuclear weapons. Publications include the quarterly *Nucleus* newsletter and reports and briefs concerning nuclear proliferation.

United States Arms Control and Disarmament Agency (ACDA)
320 Twenty-first St. NW
Washington, DC 20451
(800) 581-ACDA
fax: (202) 647-6928
Website: http://dosfan.lib.uic.edu/acda

The mission of the agency is to strengthen the national security of the United States by formulating, advocating, negotiating, implementing, and verifying effective arms control, nonproliferation, and disarmament policies, strategies, and agreements. In so doing, ACDA ensures that arms control is fully integrated into the development and conduct of U.S. national security policy. The agency publishes fact sheets on the disarmament of weapons of mass destruction as well as online records of speeches, treaties, and reports related to arms control.

For Further Reading

Books

Kaveh L. Afrasiabi, *Iran's Nuclear Program: Debating Facts Versus Fiction.* Charleston, SC: BookSurge, 2006. Written by a leading expert on Iran's foreign and nuclear affairs, this book provides insightful perspective on Iran's nuclear program.

Kurt M. Campbell, Robert J. Einhorn, and Mitchell B. Reiss, eds., *The Nuclear Tipping Point: Why States Reconsider Their Nuclear Choices.* Washington, DC: Brookings Institution, 2004. Examines the factors, both domestic and transnational, that shape nuclear policy.

Victor D. Cha and David C. Kang, *Nuclear North Korea: A Debate on Engagement Strategies.* New York: Columbia University Press, 2005. A thoughtful and analytical treatment of practical strategies for dealing with North Korea, written in a smooth and clear style.

Gordon G. Chang, *Nuclear Showdown: North Korea Takes on the World.* New York: Random House, 2006. Spotlights the world's worst regime and most egregious state proliferator of nuclear weapons.

Michael D. Evans and Jerome R. Corsi, *Showdown with Nuclear Iran: Radical Islam's Messianic Mission to Destroy Israel and Cripple the United States.* Nashville, TN: Nelson Current, 2006. Examines how Iran's president believes he has a "divine mission" to usher in the apocalypse.

Mark Hitchcock, *Iran: The Coming Crisis: Radical Islam, Oil, and the Nuclear Threat.* Sisters, OR: Multnomah, 2006. Divided into five main sections, *Iran: The Coming Crisis* contains up-to-date, thorough information on Iran's past, present, and future.

Bradley K. Martin, *Under the Loving Care of the Fatherly Leader: North Korea and the Kim Dynasty.* New York: Thomas Dunne, 2004. Offers insights into the career and character of both Kim Il-Sung and his son, Kim Jong-Il, both of whom have sought nuclear weapons for North Korea.

Albert J. Mauroni, *Where Are the WMDS? The Reality of Chem-Bio Threats on the Home Front and the Battlefront.* Annapolis, MD: Naval Institute, 2006. Offers a historical overview of chemical-biological defense issues and a policy analysis of how the U.S. government addresses the threat of weapons of mass destruction and how ground forces deal with the problem on the battlefield.

Gavan McCormack, *Target North Korea: Pushing North Korea to the Brink of Nuclear Catastrophe.* New York: Nation, 2004. Examines how North Korea's history has informed its desire for nuclear weapons.

Michael O'Hanlon and Mike M. Mochizuki, *Crisis on the Korean Peninsula: How to Deal with a Nuclear North Korea.* New York: McGraw-Hill, 2003. A comprehensive, introductory text to the conflict with North Korea over its nuclear ambitions.

Barry R. Schneider, ed., *Avoiding the Abyss: Progress, Shortfalls, and the Way Ahead in Combating the WMD Threat.* Westport, CT: Praeger, 2006. Brings together contributions from a wide range of experts to help readers understand how far the nation has come in defending against a WMD attack.

Kenneth R. Timmerman, *Countdown to Crisis: The Coming Nuclear Showdown with Iran.* New York: Crown, 2006. A veteran reporter for the *New Republic* and the *Washington Times* gives his analysis of the nuclear standoff with Iran.

James D. Torr, *Responding to Attack: The Firefighters and the Police.* San Diego: Lucent, 2003. Explores the role of firefighters, police, medics, and security agents in preparing against a WMD attack.

Al Venter, *Iran's Nuclear Option: Tehran's Quest for the Atom Bomb.* Drexel Hill, PA: Casemate, 2005. Details the extent to which Iran's weapons program has developed and the clandestine manner in which its nuclear technology has been acquired.

Norbert Vollertsen, *Inside North Korea.* New York: Encounter, 2006. A rare look inside the mysterious country.

Craig R. Whitney, ed., *The WMD Mirage: Iraq's Decade of Deception and America's False Premise for War.* PublicAffairs, 2005. Features the official report from the bipartisan Commission on the Intelligence Capabilities of the United States Regarding Weapons of Mass Destruction named by President Bush to try to prevent similar policy debacles in Iran and North Korea. Also includes the official speeches, United Nations reports, and declassified government investigation reports that show, step-by-step, how the United States got the crucial question of arms in Iraq so wrong.

Periodicals

Roger Allan, "Homeland Security's Techno War on Terror," *Electronic Design*, June 29, 2006.

Reza Aslan, "Misunderstanding Iran," *Nation*, February 28, 2005.

Gawdat Bahgat, "Nonproliferation Success: The Libyan Model," *World Affairs*, Summer 2005.

Doug Bandow, "The Hunger Artist: Starvation and Nuclear Extortion Are Kim Jong Il's Weapons of Choice," *Weekly Standard*, October 10, 2005.

Michael Barone, "The (Very) Big Lie. George W. Bush Lied About Weapons of Mass Destruction in Iraq," *U.S. News & World Report*, November 28, 2005.

Ed Blanche, "Playing with Fire," *Middle East*, February 2005.

Gloria Borger, "The Sound and the Fury," *U.S. News & World Report*, December 5, 2005.

Dorothy Boulware, "Is the USA Ready for War at Home?" *Afro-American*, July 29–August 4, 2006.

William F. Buckley Jr., "Presidential Dilemmas," *National Review*, December 5, 2005.

Michelle Ciarrocca, "Toward a New Foreign Policy," *Foreign Policy in Focus*, October 2004.

Michael Duffy, "What Would War Look Like?" *Time*, September 25, 2006.

Economist, "Bend Them, Break Them; America and a Nuclear India," October 22, 2005.

Economist, "Going Critical, Defying the World," October 21, 2006.

Trevor Findlay, "Why Treaties Work or Don't Work," *Behind the Headlines*, Autumn 2005.

Cliff Gromer and Jim Wilson, "Weapons of Mass Destruction: Easy to Build, Easy to Hide, They Pose a Greater Threat to the American Way of Life than All of Russia's Nuclear Bombs," *Popular Mechanics*, January 2005.

Robert E. Hunter, "The Iran Case: Addressing Why Countries Want Nuclear Weapons," *Arms Control Today*, December 2004.

Anatol Lieven and John Hulsman, "North Korea's Not Our Problem," *Los Angeles Times*, October 11, 2006.

Christopher Lynam, "Chemical Biological Radiological Nuclear (CBRN) Threats on International Operations," *Canadian Army Journal*, Winter 2005.

Scott MacLeod and Amany Radwan, "10 Questions for Muammar Gaddafi," *Time*, February 7, 2005.

Military & Aerospace Electronics, "New Terrorist Challenge: North Korea," July 2005.

Judith Miller, "Gadhafi's Leap of Faith," *Wall Street Journal*, May 17, 2006.

New American, "No WMD? Whatever," November 1, 2004.

New American, "What, Exactly, Is a WMD?" May 16, 2005.

Kurt Pitzer, "In the Garden of Armageddon," *Mother Jones*, September/October 2005.

Susan E. Rice, "We Need to Talk to North Korea," *Washington Post*, June 3, 2005.

Matthew Rothschild, "Runaway Train," *Progressive*, December 2004.

Robert Scheer, "Pakistan and the True WMD Threat," *Los Angeles Times*, December 7, 2004.

Benjamin Schwarz, "The Perils of Primacy," *Atlantic Monthly*, January–February 2006.

Pandy R. Sinish and Joel A. Vilensky, "WMDs in Our Backyards," *Earth Island Journal*, Winter 2005.

Fareed Zakaria, "Let Them Eat Carrots," *Newsweek*, October 23, 2006.

Web Sites

Barksdale Air Force Base: (www.barksdale.af.mil). This site is an excellent example of a nuclear base's home page and includes a phone book, photos, and organization diagrams.

Center for Biosecurity of the University of Pittsburgh Medical Center (www.upmcbiosecurity.org). An excellent site that provides information about biological threats.

The Center for Nonproliferation Studies (www.cns.miis.edu). Contains reports, tutorials, time lines, congressional testimony, and country overviews on all types of weapons of mass destruction from the largest nongovernmental organization in the United States devoted exclusively to research and training on nonproliferation issues.

Downwinders (www.downwinders.org). A research and educational foundation devoted to the residents near the Nevada test site who have been exposed to radioactive fallout from America's nuclear testing activities conducted there. Contains information about the dangers of fallout from nuclear testing, efforts to compensate victims of radiation exposure, and the future of nuclear testing in the United States.

Federation of American Scientists (www.fas.org). Provides detailed information on arms control agreements, arms sales, government secrecy, missile defense, and WMD.

The Nonproliferation Project (www.carnegieendowment.org/npp). The Carnegie Endowment for International Peace's nonproliferation project Web site offers an arsenal of information on WMDs. Find expert analysis of the WMD capabilities of countries around the world, and charts, reports, and congressional testimony on nuclear, chemical, and biological weapons and treaties.

Public Health Emergency Preparedness and Response (www.bt.cdc.gov). The Centers for Disease Control and Prevention's main site for information on biological, chemical, and radiological threats. Resources include fact sheets, news briefs, and emergency response guidelines.

Index

Ahmadinejad, Mahmoud, 71, 72, 76
Albright, Madeleine, 100
Anthrax, 10
  symptoms/effects of, 30*t*
  2001 mailings of, 9, 16
Ash, Timothy Garton, 72
Aum Shinrikyo, 12, 16

Bhopal chemical disaster (India, 1984), 10–11
Bin Laden, Osama, 11, 16
Bioweapons, 10
  symptoms/effects of, 30*t*
Bohr, Niels, 63
Bozell, L. Brent, 35
Bush, George W., 72
  Axis of Evil speech, 78
  North Korean policy of, 89–90, 96–97
  nuclear proposals of, 44, 45

Campbell, John, 15–16, 17
Carter, Jimmy, 91
Chemical weapons, 10–11
  difficulty delivering, 11
  past use of, 16
  symptoms/effects of, 30*t*
Cheney, Richard "Dick," 23–24
Clinton, Bill, 89, 94

Daily, Dell L., 19

Democratic People's Republic of Korea (DPRK)
  American opinions on, *102*
  bribery and WMDs, 99–104
  nuclear weapons and, 66–67
    facilities of, *83*
    timeline of, *95*
  sanctions against, 81–87, 88–92
  withdrawal from NPT by, 50, 103
Department of Energy, 19
Diplomacy
  Libya's WMD program and, 96
  with Iran, 79

Einstein, Albert, 63

Federal Emergency Management Agency (FEMA), 37
Federation of American (Atomic) Scientists (FAS), 63

Hussein, Saddam, 16
  U.S. support of, 78
  use of chemical weapons by, 31, 38

Improvised explosive devices (IED), 15

India, 50
International Atomic Energy
    Agency (IAEA), 43, 59
Iran, 26
    diplomacy and, 93–98
    military action and
        as effective, 69–74
        should not be taken,
            75–80
    nuclear facilities in, *73*
Iraq
    did not possess WMDs, 15,
        34–39
    Israeli bombing of nuclear
        plant in, 37
    opinion on possession of
        WMDs by, 32
    possessed WMDs, 27–33
Iraqi Survey Group, 31
Israel
    bombing of Iraqi nuclear
        plant by, 37
    possession of nuclear weapons
        by, 50

Kelly, James, 101
Khamenei, Ayatollah Ali, 72
Khan, A.Q., 43
Khomeini, Ayatollah Ruhollah,
    76
Kim Il-Sung, 100, 101
Kim Jong-Il, 90–91, 101, 104

Lugar, Richard, 58

Maples, Michael, 22–23
Mustard gas. *See* Sulfur mustard.

Negroponte, John D., 22–23,
    35, 36
Neumann, Robert E., 16–17
North Korea. *See* Democratic
    People's Republic of Korea
NPT. *See* Nuclear Non-
    Proliferation Treaty
Nuclear Non-Proliferation
    Treaty (NPT)
    can prevent spread of WMDs,
        41–47
    cannot prevent spread of
        WMDs, 48–54
    cheating on, 49
    criticism of, 65
    North Korea withdraws from,
        50, 103
Nuclear weapons
    countries abandoning, 44
    countries with, *46*
    decline in numbers of, 24,
        47
    disarmament and, 64–66
    explosions of, *60t*
    U.S. and U.S.S.R. stockpiles
        of, *23*
    world stockpiles of, 21
    worldwide testing of, *51*
Nunn, Sam, 58
Nunn-Lugar bill (1991), 58

Office of Global Radiological
    Threat Reduction, 18, 19
Opinion polls. *See* Public opin-
    ion
Oppenheimer, J. Robert, 63, 65
Osirak nuclear plant (Iraq), 37

Pakistan
  nuclear weapons and, 50
  security concerns of, 66
Powell, Colin, 90
Proliferation Security Initiative
  (PSI), 43–44
Public opinion
  on Iran and nuclear weapons,
    66
  on Iran's nuclear program, 77
  on Iraqi possession of
    WMDs, 32
  on North Korea, *102*
  war in Iraq and, 25

Al Qaeda, 11, 16

Radiological devices
  numbers recovered, 19
Rafsanjani, Hashemi, 71–72
Reeves, Stephen V., 16
Reynolds, Michael, 9
Rice, Condoleezza, 72
Rumsfeld, Donald, 19
Russia/U.S.S.R., *23*

Sanctions against North Korea
  as effective, 81–87
  as ineffective, 88–92
Sarin (nerve gas), 16, 17
  Hussein's use of, 38
  is unlikely WMD, 36
September 11 attacks (2001), 9
  G.W. Bush on, 56
  U.S. response to, 79–80
Sulfur mustard (mustard gas),
  37–38

Iraqi artillery shells with,
    28–29, 35, 36–37
  symptoms/effects of, 30*t*
Szilard, Leo, 63

Terrorism/terrorists
  access of nuclear weapons by,
    67
  fear as goal of, 18
  nuclear, 22–26
Thompson, George, 18
Tokyo subway attacks (1995),
  12, 16, 17

UN Monitoring Verification
  and Inspection Commission
  (UNMOVIC), 36
UN Security Council
  Resolution 1540, 45
  Resolution 1718, 89
United States
  aggression by, 64
  likelihood of nuclear attack
    on, 14–26
  nuclear stockpiles of, *23*

Walsch, Jim, 11–12
War in Iraq
  nuclear weapons as deterrent
    and, 53
  was justified, 31–32
Washington Post (newspaper), 72
Weapons of mass destruction
  (WMDs)
  diplomacy with North Korea
    and, 93–98
  international cooperation

and, 55–61
military actions against Iran
  and, 69–74
nothing can prevent spread
  of, 62–67
Nuclear Non-Proliferation
  Treaty
  is effective, 41–47
  is ineffective, 48–54

opinion on Iraq's possession
  of, 32
U.S. is likely to be hit by,
  14–19
U.S. is not likely to be hit by,
  20–26
Weapons of Mass Destruction
  Commission, 22
Westerman, Kurt, 18

Picture Credits

Cover photo: photos.com

AP Images, 13, 17, 25, 29, 36, 40, 43, 50, 57, 65, 68, 71, 78, 86, 91, 97, 103

Steve Zmina, 23, 30, 32, 46, 51, 60, 73, 83, 95, 102